INFERENCES FROM SOCIOLOGICAL SURVEY DATA –

A UNIFIED APPROACH

The Jossey-Bass/Elsevier
International Series

 Elsevier Scientific Publishing Company
Amsterdam

INFERENCES FROM SOCIOLOGICAL SURVEY DATA– A UNIFIED APPROACH

J.K. LINDSEY

*Groupe d'Etude des Méthodes de l'Analyse Sociologique,
Université René Descartes, Paris, France*

 Jossey-Bass Inc., Publishers
San Francisco · Washington 1973

INFERENCES FROM SOCIOLOGICAL SURVEY DATA – A UNIFIED APPROACH

by J.K. Lindsey

Copyright © by Jossey-Bass, Inc., Publishers
Elsevier Scientific Publishing Company

For the United States of America and Canada:

Jossey-Bass, Inc., Publishers
615 Montgomery Street
San Francisco, California 94111

For all other areas:

Elsevier Scientific Publishing Company
Jan van Galenstraat 335
Amsterdam, The Netherlands

Library of Congress Catalogue Card Number LC73-77068

International Standard Book Number ISBN 0-87589-184-5

Manufactured in The Netherlands

FIRST EDITION

Code 7326

The Jossey-Bass/Elsevier International Series
Progress in Mathematical Social Sciences

Other books included in this series

Lee M. Wiggins
Panel Analysis – Latent Probability Models for Attitude and Behavior Processes

Raymond Boudon
Mathematical Structures of Social Mobility

Abram DeSwaan
Coalition Theories and Cabinet Formations – a Study of Formal Theories of
Coalition Formation Applied to Nine European Parliaments after 1918

Preface

Although the use of statistical data has a long history in sociological research, perhaps dating from Durkheim's classical study of
suicide, sociologists have been slow to adopt statistical methods of
drawing inferences from such data. In some ways, sociology seems
to be attempting to follow independently the same path towards
statistical sophistication that was followed sometime previously in
the field of statistics itself, often prompted by the requirements of
biology.

An important attempt to formalize the logic of the inference-
making procedure in sociology was made by Lazarsfeld (1955,
and others 1968). Previously, simple statistical procedures, such as
correlation analysis, had been used rather uncritically. In a more
rigorously statistical vein, Simon (1954) introduced the use of
linear regression, pointing out problems related to "spurious correlation", relationships between two variables which may be explained by introducing a third. The regression approach was sys-
tematized in a number of works by Blalock (1962a,b, 1964)
applying Wright's path analysis; see also the collection of papers,
Blalock (1971). The work by Boudon (1971) provides a comprehensive description of the application of path analysis to dichotomous data. Throughout this development, attention has centred on the logic of the correct choice of and relationship between
variables, and on whether the data agree with the model. Little
attempt has been made to determine if the parameters chosen to
measure the relationships are the best or if some other contradic-
tory model is also supported by the data.

Two rather serious difficulties have arisen because this development has occurred outside the stream of statistical thought. Believing path, causal, or dependence analysis, as it has been variously called, to be distinct from regression analysis, sociologists have spent considerable time developing often complicated methods for estimating the required coefficients. Boudon (1971), for example, derives standardized regression coefficients from first principles (assuming implicitly that the observed dichotomous frequencies follow a normal distribution). In addition, deterministic rather than probabilistic models are usually assumed. Hence, estimates are obtained algebraically, often with more equations than unknown parameters, and no measure of precision is available. (If the various solutions obtained do not agree, the model is rejected.) This only adds to the unrealism of a deterministic approach to social relationships.

Many of these drawbacks may be seen to arise from the fact that the sociologist has traditionally been interested only in determining if an effect is large or small. Knowing that the effect measured is only a representation, perhaps not very accurate, of the underlying relationship being studied, he searches for a relative interpretation. Hence, also, follows the habit of dichotomizing the data, with the accompanying loss of information.

What can a modern statistical approach add to an interpretation of sociological data? In the last twenty-five years, and especially since the advent of electronic computers, the developments in mathematical statistics have been extensive. Two fields are of immediate interest to the sociologist faced with an analysis of survey data: improvements in the model describing the data and in the techniques for drawing inferences from the data given the model.

Traditionally, most statistical models used, including "least squares" linear regression, have assumed that the data follow a normal distribution, primarily for facility in making inferences. A major advance consisted in estimating a transformation which makes the data follow more closely a normal distribution. The most important work concerned with this approach is that of Box and Cox (1964). Instead of making the data fit the model, a second approach involves replacing the normal distribution by a distribution better describing the data. For the dichotomous data used by sociologists, these logistic models are described by Cox (1970). This logistic formulation of the dichotomous models will be used in this book, with extensions to cover the polychotomous case.

In the field of inference, the procedures to adopt are not so clearly defined. Three main schools of thought divide the statisticians at the present day: Neyman-Pearson (confidence intervals), Bayesian (prior probability), and Fisherian (likelihood inference). The likelihood approach has been adopted here for three main reasons; all of the information in the data about the model is used, an absolute minimum of restrictive assumptions is introduced, and one may proceed from this approach to either of the others, but not necessarily in the reverse direction. Although likelihood inference was originally proposed by Fisher in the 1920's (see Fisher, 1959a), it has lain virtually dormant until computers made feasible its application to complicated models. The paper describing likelihood inference which is most accessible to the sociologist is probably Sprott and Kalbfleisch (1965). Others include Barnard et al. (1962) and Sprott and Kalbfleisch (1969), as well as the books by Kalbfleisch (1971) and Edwards (1972).

What do these developments mean for the sociologist? The use of an improved model means that the social process under study will be described more accurately and that better insight will be provided into how that process operates. For example, the loss of information in dichotomous data may be avoided. The use of a good inference procedure means that the maximum amount of accurate information about a model may be drawn from a given set of data. For example, determining whether an effect is large or small may often be meaningless because the data provide an estimate of a large effect but also indicate that the effect could almost as plausibly not exist, or conversely that a small effect is implausibly zero.

When a complete analysis as described in this book involves many computations, and thus use of a computer, the sociologist may decide, in some situations, that the data do not warrant the expenditure. In this case, the logistic models, for example, may still be used since the amount of computation is usually about the same as for path analysis using linear regression but, in addition, all of the information in the data about the effects is used. For such cases, methods of making approximate likelihood inferences, with a minimum of calculations, are described.

From the preceding discussion, the basic concepts introduced in this book are few and straightforward: the probability distribution, mathematical model, and likelihood function. But they allow the sociologist to attack effectively such apparently diverse problems as segmentation, "causal" analysis, and social mobility processes using advanced statistical procedures.

I am very grateful to Professor R. Boudon for directing me towards a number of interesting sociological problems. I would like especially to express my appreciation to Professors D.R. Cox and J.G. Kalbfleisch, both for their invaluable tutelage in statistics and for reading the manuscript and providing many constructive comments and criticisms.

The research for this book was supported by a research fellowship from the Canada Council.

J.K. Lindsey

Contents

Introduction

In the study of social interactions, explanations or rules are not sought to describe how each individual of a group behaves. The sociologist is not concerned with determining how an individual will react in a given set of circumstances. Instead, more general relationships are developed to show that, under given circumstances, a certain proportion of individuals will do this, another proportion something else and so on, until all of the common responses or attributes have been included. Of course, as the circumstances are described and delimited more and more precisely, many individuals will be eliminated, and those remaining will give fewer different responses. In the limit, only one individual would be left if all of the circumstances, including psychological and biological as well as social factors, surrounding his situation in society could be described. With narrowly defined circumstances and few different responses, any relationship among the proportions of individuals giving different responses should be relatively simple. Conversely, if the circumstances are defined more widely, the number of different responses will be large and the relationship among the proportions complex.

In the language of probability theory, the proportions of individuals giving the various responses or having the various attributes are described by a probability distribution. The different possible responses may be given labels, often numbers, which are called the values of the response variable (the label varies depending on which individual is observed). Thus, the first task to be confronted in analyzing a set of data, the survey sample from the population, is to discover what can be said about the probability

1

distribution of the response. After introducing the basic concepts in the first chapter, this problem is discussed in detail in Chapter 2.

Throughout the book, attention will be centred on the probability distribution, *i.e.* on the proportions of individuals giving different responses, and not on the response variable, *i.e.* not on the way in which the response is described. Thus, the treatment will be very general and with a minimum of assumptions. The response variable may be qualitative (nominal), *e.g.* various answers to a question, ordered but with no measure of distance (ordinal), *e.g.* level of education, or metric, *e.g.* salary. The number of individuals giving each different response (whether an answer, an educational level, or a salary) will be analyzed and not the response itself.

If the circumstances change, one may expect that the probability distribution of responses, *i.e.* the proportion of individuals giving each response, will change. The circumstances may be altered in two ways. The definition may be widened or narrowed, *e.g.* from individuals in villages of population 500 to all individuals in a country. Of course, a probability distribution can always be defined for a given response variable, but the wider the definition of the circumstances, the more complex will be the distribution. This complexity is explained by the greater variety of individuals in the population. If this variety may be described or determined in some way (*e.g.* size of community) inclusion in the definition of circumstances is usually preferable, yielding a number of different sets of circumstances, the second type of alteration. Thus, individuals in a village of 500 may give a different distribution of responses than those in a city of a million.

The second task in the analysis of survey data is the description of how the probability distribution changes with the circumstances. A relationship among probability distributions may be called a mathematical model. In the same way that a response variable was defined, a number of independent variables or attributes may be used to describe the circumstances. Each set of circumstances is labelled by the values of one or more variables which change with the circumstances. Again, these may be nominal, ordinal, or metric. The procedures for analyzing the effects of changing conditions (independent variables) on a response distribution are discussed in Chapters 3 and 4.

Often, a preliminary task presents itself before either of the previous problems can be properly attacked. If a very large amount of data is available for a sample of individuals, some condensation must be made before analysis so that only information which is important for the question raised remains. This problem may take a number of forms, as discussed both in Chapters 2 and 5.

All of these procedures are of a very general nature and are applicable to a wide variety of data. Indeed, the term individual, itself, may refer to a group, such as a town, instead of to one person. In the final chapter, a more specialized problem is discussed, the analysis of social mobility. Although all of the procedures follow from the previous chapters, they have been specially developed for social mobility problems and are not generally applicable in other areas of sociology.

The three forms which response and independent variables may take may be related to the types of scaling defined by Torgerson (1958). Torgerson distinguishes nominal data from scaled data and then goes on to define three criteria: order, distance, and presence of a natural origin. In statistical analysis, the most important is the presence or absence of a distance or metric. Thus, nominal and ordinal data are usually treated in the same way because neither has a metric. As a mathematical convenience, metric data are divided according to whether the variable values are integers or real numbers. As will be seen in Chapters 1 and 2, in practice all metric data are actually integral or fractions multiplying integers (1.53 meters = 153 centimeters); the underlying continuous variable cannot be measured. In effect, the mathematical convenience of real numbers (used in continuous distributions) has sometimes even been a detriment when statisticians lose sight of the approximation and develop elaborate statistical theories based on theoretically continuous data which are inapplicable to the integral data actually observed.

In statistical analysis, nominal and ordinal data are usually analyzed similarly because formulation of relationships between observed values is difficult if the data have no metric, even if they are ordered. Thus, differences among variable values observed are determined, usually from some defined origin (often some form of mean). Hence, also, a natural origin is not of prime importance except in special cases, such as when a variable must be non-negative. Occasionally, as in multidimensional scaling, a variable may have a distance defined but no unidimensional ordering, *e.g.* Marxian social classes. This problem will be treated briefly in Chapters 2 and 5.

3

The analyses discussed in this book are concerned primarily with nominal variables (and hence also ordinal), but are applicable to any set of data, including metric, as a first basic approach. Indeed, if little is known about the probability and mathematical form of the data, the procedures of Chapter 2 provide an essential basis for any more sophisticated analysis of metric data.

Throughout the text, the level of mathematical and statistical sophistication has been kept to a minimum. All of the basic concepts are introduced and described as needed. An introductory knowledge of probability and statistical theory is useful but not essential. Matrix algebra has not been used and the few occurrences of integral and differential calculus may be neglected without losing the thread of the argument. Some of the more theoretical statistical aspects are briefly discussed in Appendix 1.

All statistical inferences are considered as estimation or discrimination problems. Thus, various hypotheses are compared to determine which is most plausible. No attempt is made to reject an hypothesis (model) except in comparing it with one which is more plausible. In other words, all inferences are made using the likelihood function and no tests of significance are introduced (see Appendix 1). A number of numerical examples are given to illustrate the procedures. In several cases, the data used have been adapted from other fields (usually biology); these should not be taken as representative of the problems discussed but only as illustrations of the procedures to be used.

CHAPTER 1

Basic Concepts

1.1 The Data

In the physical and biological sciences, a large part of the data analyzed is of a form which may be called continuous. Between any two values of a variable observed, another value theoretically exists if a sufficiently accurate measuring device is available. Consider, for example, the thermometer. Two possible readings are 18.3 and 18.4°C. But with a more accurate thermometer, 18.34 and 18.35°C may be read. Theoretically, although not in practice, this process may be continued ad infinitum.

By contrast, such continuous measurements are relatively rare in the social sciences. In sociology, most observations take the form of *counts* of individuals. A poll or a census is a count of the number of individuals who give various possible answers to each question posed or who fall into various defined social categories. Some proportion of all of the individuals involved will give each possible or permitted response to a question or will belong to each social category. Of course, most data of this type are complicated combinations of the above, since, for example, the individuals to whom the questions are given will be divided into various social categories, etc. Interest may lie in variations among categories in the proportions of individuals giving the responses to a question or in variations in the ways different questions are answered, or in combinations of the two. Definable and explicable relationships are sought among the actions of groups of individuals in various social situations.

As an aside, one may note that the continuous observations

may, in reality, always be considered as count data. Suppose that the thermometer, mentioned above and used in a given experiment, can be read to only one decimal place. Measurements of the form $18.3°$C. will be available and those of the form $18.34°$C. will be impossible (given the instrument). Then, counts are made of the number of times 18.3, 18.4, etc. are observed. The number 18.3 is only a label which has been observed a certain number of times. In the same way, the response y to a given question is a label or value of a variable which has been counted a certain number of times in a sample of individuals.

1.2 Probability Distributions

Consider the simplest case of count data. One question is posed to a randomly chosen homogeneous group of individuals (alike in all characteristics of interest, such as membership in any social category) with K possible responses. Only one response is allowed by each individual and all responses are mutually exclusive. Alternatively, a random sample is taken to determine the number of individuals in each of K social categories with all other important social characteristics identical for all individuals.

The assumption to be made is that, for the total population (of which the sample comprises only a small portion) from which these individuals are randomly selected, the proportion of individuals who would give each of the K responses if questioned or who belong to each of the K social categories is a fixed, although unknown, constant. For each response or category, call the fixed unknown proportion p_k. From the sample of individuals, the sociologist wishes to determine, as precisely and accurately as possible, plausible values of these proportions. Since each individual must give one of the K responses or belong to one of the K categories, the sum of the p_k's must equal one

$$\sum_k p_k = 1 \qquad (1.1)$$

Then, p_k may be interpreted as the probability that a random individual from the overall population will give response k or belong to category k.

Suppose now that, for each k, n_k individuals in the sample give response k or belong to category k. From the multinomial distribution, for the fixed values of the p_k's, if the responses of the individuals are independent, i.e. if knowing any one response provides no knowledge of the others, the probability of obtaining the observed sample (as defined by the numbers n_k) from the overall population is

$$Pr(n_1,...,n_k;p_1,...,p_k) = \frac{(\Sigma n_k)!}{\Pi n_k!} \Pi p_k^{n_k}$$ (1.2)

(Note that by definition, $0^0 = 1$ or $0 \log 0 = 0$ and also that, if an outcome is not observed ($n_k = 0$), the corresponding p_k disappears since $p_k^0 = 1$.)

At this point, the only concern is with how the sample of individuals was obtained from the population. Each p_k (the probability of an individual giving response k or belonging to category k) is fixed although unknown at the moment when the sample is taken. The most probable sample is always that with proportions of individuals the same as in the overall population. But, other possible samples will also be very nearly as probable, i.e. will occur very nearly as frequently in repeated sampling.

In the simplest case, two possible responses are available to a question or two social categories are assumed ($K = 2$). Then, eqn. (1.2) becomes

$$Pr(n_1,n_2;p_1,p_2=1-p_1) = \frac{(n_1+n_2)!}{n_1!n_2!} p_1^{n_1}(1-p_1)^{n_2}$$ (1.3)

the binomial distribution. Suppose that $p_1 = 0.5$ for the population and that the sample contains 10 individuals. The probabilities of the various possible sets of outcomes using eqn. (1.3) are given in Table 1.1. A sample with equal numbers of individuals giving the two responses ($n_1 = n_2 = 5$) will occur most frequently but samples with $n_1 = 4$ and $n_1 = 6$ will each occur almost as frequently.

TABLE 1.1

The probabilities of all possible sets of outcomes for a sample of ten individuals giving dichotomous responses following a binomial probability distribution, with $p_1 = 0.5$.

n_1	0	1	2	3	4	5	6	7	8	9	10
Pr	$\frac{1}{1024}$	$\frac{10}{1024}$	$\frac{45}{1024}$	$\frac{120}{1024}$	$\frac{210}{1024}$	$\frac{252}{1024}$	$\frac{210}{1024}$	$\frac{120}{1024}$	$\frac{45}{1024}$	$\frac{10}{1024}$	$\frac{1}{1024}$

The situation, although essentially the same, becomes more complicated for the multinomial distribution with $K > 2$.

Note that the probability distribution of eqns. (1.2) and (1.3) is a function of the observations, n_k, with the parameters, p_k, assumed fixed at some usually unknown values.

As stated above, the K possible responses or social categories may be considered as labels for the various counts or proportions. If some hypothetical or real relation exists among the labels, this may possibly be translated into a relationship among the p_k's. For example, suppose that the population of sons in a given social category is considered with respect to the social categories of fathers. One might expect that the greatest proportion of sons (the largest p_k) would have fathers of the same category, with the proportions with fathers in other categories decreasing with increased difference from the sons' category (difference to be defined in some way).

From eqn. (1.1), if $K-1$ of the p_k's are given values, the remaining p_k is determined. Thus, plausible values of $K-1$ parameters need to be determined. But from some relationship among the labels, the number of unknown parameters may possibly be reduced. Each p_k is made a function of a (usually much) smaller number of parameters, $\theta_1,...,\theta_G$, with $G < K-1$.

$$p_k = p_k(\theta_1,...,\theta_G) \qquad (k = 1,...,K) \tag{1.4}$$

With the binomial distribution of eqn. (1.3), no reduction in the number of parameters using eqn. (1.4) is possible since this distribution involves only one parameter. When $K > 2$, in order to reduce the number of parameters, some ordering of and measure of distance between the labels k is necessary. In addition, for mathematical simplicity, an infinite number of possible outcomes (labels) is often assumed, but with the probability (p_k) of many of these outcomes virtually zero. Many cases, such as the continuous observations of temperature of Section 1.1, present no difficulties. Others, such as the fathers' social categories, require further knowledge or assumptions.

Suppose that the sociologist is interested in the number of suicides in a year in various towns of similar size but with any other important characteristics assumed identical. The numbers of towns with zero, one, two, etc. suicides are counted. More towns may have zero suicides in the year than have one, more one than two, etc., but a very large number of suicides in one town (up to the limit of the population of the town) is theoretically (with extremely small probability) possible. In this example, the labels are counts as well as the observations; ordering and measuring the distance between them presents no problems.

The procedures for selecting suitable functions for eqn. (1.4) will not be discussed in this book. Sufficient to say that a suicide may be considered as a rare event, so that the probability distribution describing rare events might be chosen, the Poisson distribution; see, for example, Feller (1968, pp.156—164). Then, θ is a single parameter giving the average number of suicides per town and the function for p_k is given by

$$p_k(\theta) = \frac{\theta^k e^{-\theta}}{k!} \qquad (k = 0, 1, ..., \infty) \qquad (1.5)$$

This may be substituted into the multinomial probability distribution (1.2) to provide the probability of various sets of observations for a given value of the parameter θ. Then, the Poisson probability distribution gives

$$Pr(n_0, n_1, ...; \theta) = \frac{(\Sigma n_k)!}{\Pi n_k!} \prod_{k=0}^{\infty} \left[\frac{\theta^k e^{-\theta}}{k!} \right]^{n_k} \qquad (1.6)$$

Suppose that the actual value of θ for the overall population is 0.5. The values of $p_k(\theta = 0.5)$ from eqn. (1.5) and the probabilities of several possible combinations of results from ten towns are given in Table 1.2.

Many other combinations of results besides the twelve given in the table are possible. Note that, although an infinite number of possible outcomes is hypothesized, the probability of virtually all of these is, in effect, zero. Thus, the probability of four suicides in a town in the year, given the Poisson distribution with $\theta = 0.5$, is 0.0016. Again, as with the binomial distribution, the observed counts most closely replicating the theoretical proportions, $p_k(\theta = 0.5)$, e.g. sets A, B, and C of Table 1.2, will be most frequently observed (have the highest probability) in a sample of ten towns. But other sets will also be obtained only slightly less frequently.

This simple example illustrates the purpose of introducing a relationship among the probabilities of the possible outcomes using the functions of eqn. (1.4). The function introduces a smooth change from one p_k to the next, as shown in Fig. 1.1 for the Poisson distribution with $\theta = 0.5$. In addition, all values of p_k

TABLE 1.2

The probabilities for a selection of possible sets of outcomes for a sample of ten individuals giving responses following a Poisson probability distribution with $\theta = 0.5$.

k		0	1	2	3	4	$Pr(n_k;\theta)$
$p_k(0.5)$		0.6065	0.3033	0.0758	0.0126	0.0016	
(A)	n_k	6	3	1	0	0	0.0885
(B)	n_k	6	4	0	0	0	0.0880
(C)	n_k	7	3	0	0	0	0.1005
(D)	n_k	7	2	1	0	0	0.0758
(E)	n_k	7	1	2	0	0	0.0191
(F)	n_k	8	2	0	0	0	0.0758
(G)	n_k	8	1	1	0	0	0.0380
(H)	n_k	9	1	0	0	0	0.0302
(I)	n_k	5	4	1	0	0	0.0660
(J)	n_k	6	2	2	0	0	0.0334
(K)	n_k	4	3	3	0	0	0.0035
(L)	n_k	6	1	1	1	1	0.0001

are determined once the values of the set $\theta_1,...,\theta_G$ (in the above example, the single value, θ) are fixed.

The procedure for finding a relationship among the p_k's, as in this example, may be called probability model building. The choice of possible probability distributions (models) describing such a relationship is made from knowledge of how the data are

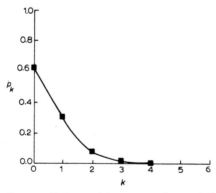

Fig. 1.1 Relationship among the probabilities, p_k, of the multinomial distribution when these are related by the Poisson probability model with $\theta = 0.5$.

10

generated. If one possible distribution is chosen, the sociologist will want to know if the observed data support the choice, and if not what other distribution might be plausible. If more than one is chosen, he will want to know which is most plausible for the data. The problem of the choice of possible distributions is beyond the scope of this book; the problem of plausibility is considered in Chapter 2. But, for the most part, an analysis of data will be developed for which no probability distribution is assumed other than the multinomial.

Another possible method exists for reducing the number of parameters, p_k, in the multinomial distribution (1.2). Suppose that an open question is posed so that the individuals are not limited to one of a certain number of responses or that, in the same way, the number of social categories is not limited. Then, the number of different observed responses or categories will vary depending on what sample of individuals happens to be chosen from the population. A different label and probability (p_k) is assigned to each possible response or category, even those not observed in the sample. Of course, as noted above, any label not observed will not appear in the probability distribution (1.2) for the sample since $p_k^0 = 1$. Some responses or social categories will be very similar and others very different. The sociologist will want to group the responses or categories without distorting the original observed probability distribution, hence reducing the number of labels and parameters. In this way, the number of observed outcomes may be reduced from K to say K'. With a clear metric and ordering relating the labels, grouping will be straightforward. For example, in the temperature example of Section 1.1 with measurements to one decimal, one might begin by grouping 18.3 and 18.4, 18.5 and 18.6, etc. In contrast, the definition of similarity of responses to a question is much more difficult. This problem of grouping labels will be considered in detail in Chapter 2 and further in Section 5.5.

1.3 Determination of Plausible Values of the Parameters

The above discussion has been concerned with the form which data may take (counts) and with how it is generated (by some probability distribution or model). The probability distribution has been considered to be completely specified and fixed at the moment or over the time period when the data are observed. But,

11

of course, the sociologist does not know the specification of the probability distribution (*i.e.* whether it is Poisson, normal, etc.) nor at what values the parameters are fixed. He has only the observed data and wishes to discover what these can tell him about the probability distribution.

Assume that the sociologist has no previous quantifiable information telling him that one value of a parameter is preferable to another (*e.g.* $p_1 = 0.4$ is twice as preferable as $p_1 = 0.35$) for all possible parameter values, or that one of the probability distributions which he has hypothesized is preferable (*e.g.* the Poisson distribution is twice as preferable as some other distribution). In addition, assume that the number of different possible outcomes (labels or variable values) is not limited so that they do not necessarily all appear in the sample observed (*e.g.* some individuals not questioned might have given responses to an open question which the sociologist has not thought of and which do not appear among the observed responses). This second assumption is a generalization containing the special case in which the number of different possible outcomes is fixed; it does not affect the probability distribution of the observed data (except that the sum of those p_k appearing in the function will be less than unity), since, as observed in Section 1.2, any label with no observations does not appear in the distribution ($p_k{}^0 = 1$). All outcomes are also assumed independent of each other.

If the simple case for count data with a homogeneous group of individuals is considered, the probability of the observed data is given by eqn. (1.2) where K may be any number at least as large as the total number of different labels observed (and might, for convenience, be made infinite). But, of course, the sociologist is now in a different situation than in the previous section where he was assumed to know the values of the p_k's. Here, the values of the n_k's have been observed and are thus known, and he wishes to determine what values of the p_k's are consistent with these observed counts. Hence, eqn. (1.2) is no longer a function of the n_k's to be observed for given, fixed values of the p_k's but is a function of possible values of the p_k's for the observed n_k's. *This is no longer a probability function.* As a function of the unknown parameters, p_k, eqn. (1.2) is known as the likelihood function, and is written as

$$L_M(p_1,...,p_K; n_1,...,n_K) = C \prod_k p_k{}^{n_k} \qquad (1.7)$$

where C is a constant, not a function of the p_k's. As a simplification, $L_M(p_1,...,p_K; n_1,...,n_K)$ is usually written $L_M(p_1,...,p_K)$ but one should keep in mind that this L_M holds only for the given observed set of values, $n_1,...,n_K$.

From eqn. (1.7), the likelihood of a set of values of p_k for given data $n_1,...,n_K$ is the probability of observing that data if the set of parameter values are the true values. A set of values of p_k is considered more likely or plausible (but *not* probable) or to have more support from the data than another set if the first set makes the observed data more probable, *i.e.* if the likelihood is larger. Since, for example using eqn. (1.5) of the Poisson distribution, sets of values of the p_k's are defined for any probability distribution, this measure of plausibility includes comparison among probability models.

Consider the simplest possible example, with two observed labels, the binomial distribution of eqn. (1.3). The corresponding likelihood function is

$$L_B(p_1, p_2 = 1 - p_1) = C\, p_1{}^{n_1}(1 - p_1)^{n_2} \qquad (1.8)$$

with only one parameter, p_1, unknown. Suppose that, in a sample of ten individuals, four have label one. Then, $n_1 = 4$, $n_2 = 6$ and the likelihood function becomes

$$L_B(p_1) = C\, p_1{}^4 (1 - p_1)^6 \qquad (1.9)$$

The most plausible or best supported value of p_1 is the value which makes $L_B(p_1)$ greatest for the given observations. In order to find the maximum, set the first derivative of $L_B(p_1)$ with respect to p_1 equal to zero and solve the resulting equation. But since $\log L_B(p_1)$ is a monotone function of $L_B(p_1)$, it will have the same maximum and simplifies the calculations

$$\log L_B(p_1) = \log C + 4 \log p_1 + 6 \log (1 - p_1)$$

$$\frac{d \log L_B(\hat{p}_1)}{d\hat{p}_1} = \frac{4}{\hat{p}_1} - \frac{6}{1 - \hat{p}_1} = 0$$

The solution, $\hat{p}_1 = 0.4$, is the maximum likelihood estimate of p_1. Of course, this result is to be expected intuitively since it is just the proportion of individuals in the sample with label one. For the multinomial distribution, the maximum likelihood estimates, $\hat{p}_k$, of the proportions, p_k, of individuals in the overall population with the various labels will be the observed proportions, $n_k / \Sigma n_k$,

13

in the sample. No other set of values of the p_k's can make the observed data more probable if the only restriction is $\Sigma p_k \leqslant 1$.

In general, these maximum likelihood estimates of the population proportions will not be the true values which generated the observed data and hence will be of somewhat limited value (see, for example, Sprott and Kalbfleisch, 1969). From Table 1.1, they will be the true values only if the most probable sample occurs, but other samples will also occur very frequently. The sociologist wishes to know which other values of the parameters might also have plausibly generated the observed data. Consider, for example, the outcomes of Table 1.1, generated by a binomial distribution with $p_1 = 0.5$. As stated in Section 1.2, the observation $n_1 = 4$ is quite probable, but this gives a maximum likelihood estimate of $\hat{p}_1 = 0.4$. What is the relative plausibility of the value $p_1 = 0.5$ as compared with $\hat{p}_1$ for these data? Remember that the true value, $p_1 = 0.5$, is not actually known. To make this relative comparison, consider the ratio of likelihoods for the two values of p_1 using eqn. (1.9)

$$R_B(p_1 = 0.5) = \frac{(0.5)^4(0.5)^6}{(0.4)^4(0.6)^6} = 0.817$$

The value $p_1 = 0.5$ makes the observed data approximately 4/5 as probable as does the maximum likelihood estimate, $\hat{p}_1 = 0.4$, or has relative likelihood $R_B = 0.817$. In general, the relative likelihood function for the binomial distribution is given by

$$R_B(p_1) = \frac{p_1{}^{n_1}(1-p_1)^{n_2}}{\hat{p}_1{}^{n_1}(1-\hat{p}_1)^{n_2}} \tag{1.10}$$

where $\hat{p}_1$, the maximum likelihood estimate, is calculated from the observed data. Since the denominator gives the maximum value of the likelihood function, $R_B(p_1)$ varies between zero and one and provides a metric for determining the relative plausibility of any value of p_1 between zero and one. For the example considered above, with $n_1 = 4$, $n_2 = 6$, function (1.10) is plotted in Fig. 1.2. From the relative likelihood, $R_B(p_1 = 0.5) = 0.817$, one may conclude that $p_1 = 0.5$ is one of the values of p_1 which is relatively plausible for the observed data.

As the number of individuals sampled is increased, the relative likelihood graph becomes much narrower, i.e. the range of plausible values of the parameter becomes much smaller and inferences

14

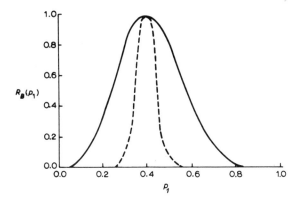

Fig. 1.2 Graph of the relative likelihood function for the binomial distribution when the maximum likelihood estimate is $\hat{p}_1 = 0.4$. The solid line is for a sample of ten individuals ($n_1 = 4$, $n_2 = 6$) and the broken line, a sample of 100 ($n_1 = 40$, $n_2 = 60$), showing the increase in precision of the estimate with increased sample size.

about the parameter are more precise. Consider, for example, the same true probability distribution with $p_1 = 0.5$ but with 100 individuals sampled. In order to have the same proportion of individuals with label one in the sample, n_1 must be 40. But

$$Pr(n_1 = 40, n_2 = 60; p_1 = 0.5) = 0.0109$$

whereas

$$Pr(n_1 = 4, n_2 = 6; p_1 = 0.5) = 0.2051$$

as compared with the observations with largest probability, respectively

$$Pr(n_1 = 50, n_2 = 50; p_1 = 0.5) = 0.0796$$

and

$$Pr(n_1 = 5, n_2 = 5; p_1 = 0.5) = 0.2461$$

Thus for $p_1 = 0.5$, $n_1 = 40$ in a sample of 100 will occur about 1/8 as many times as the most probable sample, $n_1 = 50$, whereas $n_1 = 4$ in a sample of 10 will occur about 4/5 as many times as the most probable sample, $n_1 = 5$. These results will be reflected by the relative likelihood; if a relatively rare event is observed, the plausibility of the true (although unknown) parameter value will be small. For the sample $n_1 = 40$, $n_2 = 60$, the relative likelihood

15

of $p_1 = 0.5$ is

$$R_B(p_1=0.5) = \frac{(0.5)^{40}(0.5)^{60}}{(0.4)^{40}(0.6)^{60}} = 0.133$$

which, although not very implausible, is much more so than the corresponding result for a sample of ten individuals given above.

The results for the two sample sizes are summarized in Fig. 1.2 where the two relative likelihood functions have been plotted. From these graphs, one may make a statement such as that the 0.1 likelihood intervals for p_1 for the two samples are respectively $0.13 \leqslant p_1 \leqslant 0.72$ and $0.30 \leqslant p_1 \leqslant 0.51$. These intervals are interpreted to mean that all values of p_1 within their limits (a) make the observed data at least one tenth as probable as that value (the maximum likelihood estimate) making them most probable, or (b) have a relative likelihood of at least one tenth. Note that no probability statement is made about values of the parameter, nor about the interval which has been constructed.

All of these procedures for the binomial distribution are directly applicable to the multinomial likelihood function (1.7). The only problem arises in attempting to represent the relative likelihood function in this multiparameter situation by a graph such as that of Fig. 1.2. But, this is purely a visual problem. The relative likelihood function for the multinomial distribution is

$$R_M(p_1,...,p_K) = \prod_k \frac{p_k^{n_k}}{\hat{p}_k^{n_k}} \tag{1.11}$$

with maximum likelihood estimates given by

$$\hat{p}_k = \frac{n_k}{n_.} \qquad (k = 1, 2, ..., K) \tag{1.12}$$

where $n_. = \Sigma\, n_k$, the total number of individuals sampled.

Note that at this stage in the determination of plausibility of parameters, no assumption has been made about degree of similarity of labels (metric) or about ordering of the labels, $k = 1,2,...,K$. Rearrangement of the labelling system does not affect the results. For example, interchanging the labels 1 and 2 for the binomial distribution gives $n_2 = 4$, $n_1 = 6$, $\hat{p}_2 = 1-\hat{p}_1 = 0.4$. Only when the number of parameters is to be reduced, either by introducing another probability model using eqn. (1.4), or by grouping labels, must these restrictions be introduced.

16

Let us now consider this case for the Poisson distribution of Section 1.2. From Table 1.2, suppose that $n_0 = 6$, $n_1 = 3$, $n_2 = 1$, $n_k = 0$ for $k > 2$, with $n. = 10$ (set A). This yields a multinomial likelihood function with two parameters (labelled from zero instead of from one).

$$L_M(p_0,p_1,p_2) = C\, p_0{}^6 p_1{}^3 p_2{}^1$$

from eqn. (1.7). The maximum likelihood estimates are $\hat{p}_0 = 0.6$, $\hat{p}_1 = 0.3$, $\hat{p}_2 = 0.1$ and the relative likelihood function is

$$R_M(p_0,p_1,p_2) = \frac{p_0{}^6 p_1{}^3 p_2{}^1}{(0.6)^6(0.3)^3(0.1)^1} \qquad (\Sigma p_k \leqslant 1)$$

from eqn. (1.11). From eqn. (1.6), the likelihood function for the Poisson distribution is

$$L_P(\theta) = C \left[\frac{\theta^0 e^{-\theta}}{0!}\right]^6 \left[\frac{\theta^1 e^{-\theta}}{1!}\right]^3 \left[\frac{\theta^2 e^{-\theta}}{2!}\right]^1$$

$$= C\, \frac{\theta^5 e^{-10\theta}}{2}$$

from which the maximum likelihood estimate may be derived

$$\frac{d \log L_P(\hat{\theta})}{d\hat{\theta}} = \frac{d(5 \log \hat{\theta} - 10\hat{\theta})}{d\hat{\theta}} = \frac{5}{\hat{\theta}} - 10 = 0$$

yielding $\hat{\theta} = 0.5$. Then, from eqn. (1.5), $p_0(\hat{\theta}) = 0.6065$, $p_1(\hat{\theta}) = 0.3033$, $p_2(\hat{\theta}) = 0.0758$. Since the Poisson distribution hypothesizes an infinite number of possible labels, these three estimates do not sum to one. Of course, all of the other values of $p_k(\hat{\theta})$ for $k > 2$ may be calculated for the labels not observed in the sample, i.e., in the example, for all towns with more than two suicides in the year, but since the corresponding $n_k = 0$, these factors, $p_k{}^{n_k}$, do not appear in the relative likelihood function. The substitution of the estimates of the p_k's into the relative likelihood function yields

$$R_M(\text{Poisson with } \hat{\theta}) = \frac{(0.6065)^6(0.3033)^3(0.0758)^1}{(0.6)^6(0.3)^3(0.1)^1} = 0.835$$

indicating, as might be expected, that the Poisson probability model with $\hat{\theta} = 0.5$ is very plausible for this set of data.

With set K of data from Table 1.2, $n_0 = 4$, $n_1 = 3$, $n_2 = 3$ yielding $\hat{\theta} = 0.9$ and R_M (Poisson with $\hat{\theta}=0.9$) = 0.189. Here, the most plausible estimate of θ for the Poisson distribution (1.6) is $\hat{\theta} = 0.9$, whereas the true value was set at $\theta = 0.5$. Then, R_M(Poisson with $\theta=0.5$) = 0.052, showing that this set of data is not as typical of data generated by a Poisson distribution with $\theta = 0.5$ (a relatively rare combination of Poisson events has occurred). Thus, the value R_M(Poisson with $\hat{\theta}$) must be interpreted with care. It gives the relative plausibility of the Poisson distribution making the data most probable as compared with the probability distribution in general (the multinomial) making the given data most plausible, and not the relative plausibility for the Poisson distribution in general. This problem may be seen from another viewpoint. The multinomial distribution of the denominator requires the estimation of two parameters, p_1 and p_2, whereas the Poisson distribution of the numerator of the relative likelihood requires the estimation of only one parameter. Hence, when considering the loss of plausibility in adopting the Poisson distribution, the gain in simplicity by reduction in parameter number, as well as other theoretical sociological reasons for adopting the Poisson model of rare events, must be taken into account.

If the Poisson distribution is considered plausible from the data or is adopted because of previous analysis of similar data (in which case, verification of plausibility for the present set of data is always desirable), the sociologist will wish to determine which values of the parameter θ are plausible, as was done for the binomial distribution above. The function, R_M (Poisson with θ) may be used, but since its range does not extend to one but only to R_M(Poisson with $\hat{\theta}$), normalization may be useful. For the Poisson distribution, the relative likelihood function may be defined as

$$R_P(\theta) = \frac{R_M(\text{Poisson with } \theta)}{R_M(\text{Poisson with } \hat{\theta})} \qquad (1.13)$$

Since the denominator of R_M(Poisson with θ) is the same for all values of θ, including $\hat{\theta}$, eqn. (1.13) becomes

$$R_P(\theta) = \prod_k \left[\frac{p_k(\theta)}{p_k(\hat{\theta})}\right]^{n_k} = \prod_k \left[\frac{\theta^k e^{-\theta}}{\hat{\theta}^k e^{-\hat{\theta}}}\right]^{n_k} \qquad (1.14)$$

from eqns. (1.11) and (1.5). Of course, this relative likelihood function could have been derived directly from eqn. (1.6) in the same way that the corresponding function R_B (1.10) for the binomial distribution was derived from eqn. (1.3).

18

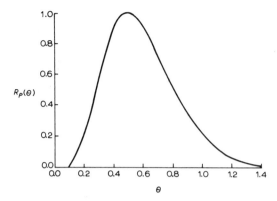

Fig. 1.3 Graph of the relative likelihood function for the Poisson distribution when the sample contains ten individuals ($n_0 = 6$, $n_1 = 3$, $n_2 = 1$) and the maximum likelihood estimate is $\hat{\theta} = 0.5$.

Consider again the data, $n_0 = 6$, $n_1 = 3$, $n_2 = 1$ for which $\hat{\theta} = 0.5$. The relative likelihood function for the Poisson distribution, as plotted in Fig. 1.3, may be treated in the same way as that for the binomial distribution to determine which values of the parameter θ may be considered plausible given the observed data and the Poisson assumption. In other words, the relative plausibilities of various average rates of suicide per town per year are obtained from the data. But the additional Poisson assumption must be kept in mind since plausibility statements using the binomial and multinomial likelihood functions do not require a metric or an ordering of the labels of the observed counts.

The procedures outlined in this section provide a basis for the analysis of any sample of data which is small in comparison with the size of the hypothesized population under study. If a large portion of the individuals in a population have been sampled, finite survey sampling techniques may be used to provide more precise inferences. These procedures will not be discussed in this book, but see, for example, the discussion following the election example of Section 4.3. Thus, the first step is to hypothesize a probability distribution (or, if necessary, several) which may have generated the data and then to verify that this distribution adequately describes the observed data. If no other distribution presents itself, the multinomial distribution with its absolute minimum of assumptions, that each possible outcome or label is independent with probability p_k of occurring, is used. This book is primarily concerned with this situation.

19

The relationship of the likelihood methods of making inferences outlined in this section to the more classical approaches, for example using normal distribution theory and Neyman—Pearson confidence intervals or Bayesian procedures, is discussed briefly in Appendix 1.

1.4 Mathematical Models

Up until this point, only the simplest case of data from a group of individuals homogeneous in all pertinent aspects, except the one which is to be measured, has been considered. But most data gathered are much more complex. For example, the sociologist may pose the same question to groups of individuals belonging to a number of different social categories in order to determine how the distribution of responses varies among the categories. In other words, each homogeneous population from which a group is sampled is assumed to have a different probability distribution describing the frequency with which the various possible outcomes or labels may be observed. Then, a mathematical model will describe the relationship among these distributions.

In the analysis of sociological survey data, a second important source of difference in responses arises from individuals interpreting differently the same question or giving the same answer for different reasons. For example, the sociologist may pose questions to obtain information on political opinions but some answers may be given for, say, economic reasons (the latest increase in milk prices). This problem raises interesting logical problems: further questions posed to clarify the response lead into a vicious circle. Thus, two forms of conditions, explicit and implicit, influence the distributions of sociological responses. The sociologist must attempt to explain both as accurately as possible in order to construct statistical models of social behaviour.

As with the relationship among possible outcomes within a homogeneous group described by a probability model, the mathematical model may or may not assume some relationships of similarity and ordering among the groups. Suppose that I homogeneous groups are considered so that p_{ik} gives the proportion of individuals in the overall homogeneous population, i, giving response k, and n_{ik} the corresponding observed count in a sample. If the observations for the various groups are independent, the relative likelihood function for making inferences about mathematical models will be

$$R_M(p_{ik}, i=1,...,I, k=1,...,K) = \prod_i \prod_k (p_{ik}/\hat{p}_{ik})^{n_{ik}} \qquad (1.15)$$

from eqn. (1.11), where $\Sigma p_{ik} = 1$ (all i) and $\hat{p}_{ik} = n_{ik}/n_{i.}$ (all i,k; $n_{i.} = \Sigma_k n_{ik}$). Each homogeneous population has the same basic distribution, the multinomial, but with the (unknown) values of the parameters varying among the groups.

Suppose that the sociologist is interested in determining the plausibility of a difference in the distribution of outcomes among the various groups. Consider, for example, the hypothesis of no difference in distribution among groups. In eqn. (1.15), $p_{ik} = p_k$ (all i,k), i.e. the proportion of responses to outcome k does not vary among the groups, and $\hat{p}_k = n_{.k}/n_{..}$ so that

$$R_M(p_{ik}=\hat{p}_k) = \prod_i \prod_k (n_{.k}n_{i.}/n_{..}n_{ik})^{n_{ik}} \qquad (1.16)$$

where

$$n_{.k} = \sum_i n_{ik}, \qquad n_{i.} = \sum_k n_{ik}, \qquad n_{..} = \sum_i \sum_k n_{ik}$$

Equation (1.16) gives the relative likelihood that the responses to the question posed are independent of the social category to which an individual belongs as opposed to the hypothesis of dependence of response on category. In effect, the observed counts form an $I \times K$ table with elements n_{ik} and marginals $n_{i.}, n_{.k}$. Under the hypothesis of independence between rows and columns, the elements would be $n_{.k}n_{i.}/n_{..}$. Equation (1.16) gives the product of the ratio of the elements under the hypothesis of independence to the observed counts, raised to the power n_{ik}. If this hypothesis of independence is found to be implausible (R_M is very small) i.e. if differences in the distribution of responses among groups are plausible, the sociologist may wish to determine among which groups the greatest differences exist, by repeating the procedure using sub-collections of the groups. Such problems will be discussed in detail in Chapter 4.

If some other probability model is to be used, exactly the same methods are applicable. For example, with the Poisson model, one might hypothesize $\theta_i = \theta$ (all i) and proceed as will be discussed below.

The general problem of determining plausibility of differences in distributions of outcomes among homogeneous groups will be considered in detail in Chapters 3 and 4. Although this problem is not always considered as involving a mathematical model, in these chapters it will be placed in the general framework of mathematical models.

A mathematical model is usually considered to describe a quantitative relationship among groups of individuals. But, in order for this to be true, the additional assumption of similarity and of order among the groups must be introduced. If two groups are similar or close together in the ordering, one may hypothesize that their probability distributions will also be similar (or more precisely, the parameters of their distributions), as compared to groups which are relatively dissimilar.

At this point, the usefulness of reducing the number of parameters becomes evident. With one parameter in the probability model, as with the binomial and Poisson distributions, the definition of a mathematical relationship, describing how the parameter changes with the group, is relatively straightforward (although the selection of a suitable one may not be). With the $K-1$ parameters of the multinomial probability model, the function becomes more complex. This problem will be considered in Chapter 4 and a special case discussed in Chapter 6.

As a simple example of the construction of a mathematical model, take the binomial distribution with relative likelihood function.

$$R_B(p_{i1}, i=1,...,I) = \prod_i \left[\frac{p_{i1}}{\hat{p}_{i1}}\right]^{n_{i1}} \left[\frac{1-p_{i1}}{1-\hat{p}_{i1}}\right]^{n_{i2}} \tag{1.17}$$

where $p_{i2} = 1-p_{i1}$, $\hat{p}_{i1} = n_{i1}/n_{i.}$. Some function, $g_i(\phi_{i1},...,\phi_{iH})$, of a new, unknown set of parameters is selected to describe how p_{i1} changes among the groups. Suppose that the relationship chosen is

$$p_{i1} = g_i(\phi_{i1},...,\phi_{iH})$$

But, in eqn. (1.17), since p_{i1} is symmetric with $1-p_{i1}$, the relationship chosen might as well have been

$$p_{i2} = (1-p_{i1}) = g_i(\phi_{i1},...,\phi_{iH})$$

Thus, some relationship symmetric in p_{i1} and in $1-p_{i1}$ such as

$$p_{i1}/(1-p_{i1}) = g_i(\phi_{i1},...,\phi_{iH})$$

appears to be more reasonable. But, suppose that the function $g_i(\phi_{i1},...,\phi_{iH})$ is estimated as a negative number for some set of data. Either p_{i1} or $(1-p_{i1})$ must be estimated as negative, which is not admissible since both are proportions or probabilities lying between zero and one. Then, a function such as

$$\log[p_{i1}/(1-p_{i1})] = g_i(\phi_{i1},...,\phi_{iH}) \qquad \text{(all } i) \qquad (1.18)$$

seems to be most useful. In addition, in this form the maximum likelihood estimates, $\hat{\phi}_{ih}$, will contain all of the information in the data if $g_i(\phi_{i1},...,\phi_{iH})$ is a linear function of the parameters ϕ_{ih}.

The models of form (1.18) may be compared with the other forms in a simple example, when $g_i(\phi_{i1},...,\phi_{iH}) = \phi_1 + \phi_2 x_i$. For example, the first form listed above, linear in p_{i1}, gives a regression curve of the shape shown in Fig. 1.4, whereas eqn. (1.18) gives the curve shown in Fig. 1.5. The first model corresponds to that traditionally used by sociologists, for example Boudon (1971), in the analysis of dichotomous data. But in most cases, the second seems more reasonable at least as a first approximation. Rasch (1960, 1961) provides justification for this model in some specific social science problems.

Equation (1.18) may be solved for p_{i1}.

$$p_{i1} = \frac{\exp[g_i(\phi_{i1},...,\phi_{iH})]}{1 + \exp[g_i(\phi_{i1},...,\phi_{iH})]}$$

and this function substituted into the relative likelihood function (1.17) so that the plausibility of the mathematical model (1.18) may be determined and of various values of the parameters ϕ_{ih}, if the model is acceptable.

Of course, $g_i(\phi_{i1},...,\phi_{iH})$ will be chosen according to a number

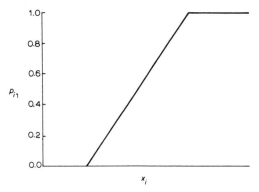

Fig. 1.4 Form of the regression fitted when the equation is a linear function of the proportion calculated from dichotomous data: $p_{i1} = \phi_1 + \phi_2 x_i$.

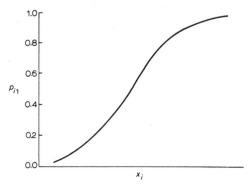

Fig. 1.5 Form of the regression fitted, for the same fictitious data as Fig. 1.4, when the equation is a linear function of the log odds ratio calculated from dichotomous data (logistic model): $\log(p_{i1}/p_{i2}) = \phi_1 + \phi_2 x_i$.

of criteria. The function should be theoretically acceptable and interpretable for the sociologist. Mathematical tractability may be required if high-powered numerical tools (such as an electronic computer) are not readily available, *e.g.* linearity of the parameters ϕ_{ih}. And the function should be as simple as possible, usually involving a smaller number of parameters than previously existed, *i.e.* than the I parameters p_{i1}.

Consider the simplest case, where $g_i(\phi_{i1},....,\phi_{iH}) = C$, a constant for all values of i, in eqn. (1.18). Then,

$$p_{i1} = \frac{e^C}{1 + e^C}$$

which may be relabelled $p_{i1} = p_1$ before substitution into the relative likelihood function (1.17). This mathematical model hypothesizes no differences in response among groups. It yields the equivalent for the binomial distribution to eqn. (1.16) for the multinomial distribution.

If, within the homogeneous groups, some reduction in the number of parameters has been possible by either method mentioned in Section 1.2, the corresponding likelihood function should be used. If combination of the counts from a number of labels using the procedures to be described in Chapter 2 has been found possible, the multinomial likelihood function with the reduced number of parameters will be used. Or, if some other probability model such as the Poisson of Section 1.3 has been found plausible within the groups, this should be used.

24

If the same probability model is not found to be plausible for all of the groups, the probability distribution is automatically different among groups. In this case, the I groups may be divided into sub-collections and the relationship among distributions for the groups within each sub-collection analyzed separately using the appropriate probability model.

Suppose that the Poisson distribution has been found plausible for all groups. The parameter θ_i will vary with the group and the relative likelihood function will be

$$R_P(\phi_1,...,\phi_I) = \prod_i \prod_k \left[\frac{\phi_i{}^k e^{-\theta_i}}{\hat{\theta}_i{}^k e^{-\hat{\theta}_i}} \right]^{n_{ik}} \tag{1.19}$$

from eqn. (1.14) where

$$\hat{\theta}_i = \sum_{k=0}^{K} k\, n_{ik} \bigg/ \sum_{k=0}^{K} n_{ik}$$

is estimated separately for each group.

In the more complex situation of this section, sufficient data are often not available within each group to determine if a reduction in parameter number from the full multinomial model is possible. If the sociologist wishes to make such a reduction, he must either use information from previous research with similar data or take a preliminary sample from only one or a small number of the groups under consideration, determine a plausible probability model, and assume that this model holds for the other groups (with different parameter values, of course). Otherwise, a normal theory analysis (e.g. least squares linear regression or analysis of variance) is applied using the label values instead of the frequencies, if these variables have a metric.

Suppose that the example of counts of suicides in towns during a year is extended to various groups of towns with different sizes of populations and that the Poisson model has been found plausible within the various groups. The relative likelihood function for making inferences was given in eqn. (1.19). The parameter θ_i measures the average number of suicides per town per year within each group of towns and the hypothesis is that this average suicide rate varies with the size of the town. Some function, $g_i(\phi_{i1}, ...,\phi_{iH})$, is sought describing this relationship. With the same reasoning as above for the binomial distribution, since the parameter

θ_i must be greater than zero,

$$\log \theta_i = g_i(\phi_{i1}, ..., \phi_{iH}) \tag{1.20}$$

might be selected and the function substituted into the relative likelihood function (1.19) eliminating the parameters θ_i. Suppose that the average number of suicides per year is in direct relationship with the population x_i of the town concerned. One possible mathematical model which might be selected for simplicity is

$$\log \theta_i = \phi_1 + x_i \phi_2 \tag{1.21}$$

so that the I parameters θ_i are reduced to two.

The substitution of this mathematical model into the Poisson probability model obtained by generalizing eqn. (1.6) yields the relative likelihood function

$$R_P(\phi_1, \phi_2) = \prod_i \prod_k \frac{\{\exp [k(\phi_1 + x_i \phi_2)]\}\{\exp [-\exp (\phi_1 + x_i \phi_2)]\}}{\hat{\theta}_i^k e^{-\hat{\theta}_i}} \tag{1.22}$$

from eqn. (1.19). From this function (or equivalently from the corresponding likelihood function), the maximum likelihood estimates of ϕ_1 and ϕ_2 may be obtained and inferences made about the plausibility of this mathematical model (1.21) for the observed set of data and then about various values of the parameters, ϕ_1 and ϕ_2.

Many mathematical models other than that of eqn. (1.21) might have been chosen for this analysis. Indeed, in some situations

$$\theta_i = \phi'_1 + x_i \phi'_2 \tag{1.23}$$

may seem more reasonable and may prove more plausible for the observed data. But care must be taken if one wishes to predict the suicide rate for a town, for example, with population x_i smaller than any in the sample from which ϕ'_1 and ϕ'_2 have been estimated since a negative suicide rate may result. (Indeed, this may occur for some of the x_i actually observed if this model is poor.) For example, suppose that $\hat{\phi}'_1 = -1.0$ and $\hat{\phi}'_2 = 0.0005$. For towns of 10,000, the average number of suicides per year would be predicted to be $\hat{\theta} = 4$ but for towns of 1000, $\hat{\theta} = -0.5$ suicides. In other words, extrapolation outside the range of a sample will often be much safer using a mathematical model such as eqn. (1.18) or eqn. (1.20) than with one such as eqn. (1.23).

The plausibility of the mathematical models (1.21) and (1.23) may, of course, be compared using the relative likelihood function. Corresponding to eqn. (1.22), a relative likelihood function is constructed for mathematical model (1.23) from eqn. (1.19). The maximum likelihood estimates, $\hat{\phi}_j$ and $\hat{\phi}_j'$, are obtained and substituted into the corresponding relative likelihood functions. The two values of relative likelihood obtained give the relative plausibility of the two mathematical models, with values of R_P close to one indicating high plausibility of the model. This measure of plausibility is only valid for the observed data and gives no indication of extrapolation ability.

If a mathematical model has been found to be supported by the data and is acceptable to the sociologist, plausible values of the parameters are determined using the relative likelihood function. As in Section 1.3, when the Poisson probability model was found to be supported, the relative likelihood function may be normalized in the same manner as with eqn. (1.13). For example, eqn. (1.22) may be divided by $R_P(\hat{\phi}_1, \hat{\phi}_2)$ to yield the relative likelihood function for the Poisson probability model incorporating mathematical model (1.21). This combination of models may be called a statistical model.

The reader may, at this point, have realized that a general theory of regression analysis has been constructed without including the restricting assumption that the data follow a normal distribution. Indeed, if the Poisson probability model is replaced by the normal distribution, all of the preceding discussion holds and the normal theory ("least squares") regression analysis results. But when approached from the point of view of this chapter, any theoretically suitable probability distribution may be used provided that it is found to be compatible with the observed data, i.e. plausible using the procedures of Section 1.3.

CHAPTER 2

Analysis Within a Group: Probability Models

2.1 The Problem of Combining Responses

Throughout this chapter, attention will be restricted to the simple case of analyzing the distribution of outcomes within a single group of individuals. A population of individuals which is sufficiently homogeneous in all aspects except that to be measured is assumed. In general, an infinite number of different possible outcomes may be assumed for the aspect observed, as labelled by k, with a proportion p_k of individuals in the overall population corresponding to each label or outcome. The ability to distinguish among different outcomes is assumed limited by the measuring device (e.g. the question posed and the limits of language used in answering). A finite sample of individuals is chosen at random from the population and their labels or outcomes recorded. With a finite number, K, of different outcomes observed in the sample of n individuals ($K \leqslant n$) and with n_k ($k=1,...,K$; $\Sigma n_k = n$) individuals in the sample having label or outcome k, the probability of observing the given sample is given by eqn. (1.2) and the corresponding relative likelihood function, R_M, by eqn. (1.11).

But suppose that the measuring device can distinguish very fine differences among labels. For example, a question is posed with no restriction (such as yes/no or select one of five) in possible answers. Virtually all of the answers may be found to be slightly different in some respect. Most of the observed counts will be $n_k = 1$ and there seems to be little information about a possible distribution applicable in or comparable with other situations, *i.e.* other homogeneous groups. The sociologist will want to group the responses into a small number of basically different types. Two questions arise: which responses to group together and how many basic types to use?

The first question depends on some measure of similarity among observed outcomes so that outcomes which are most similar or close together in an ordering will be grouped together first. The second question is more complicated, so that, to simplify in a first approach, the case of strictly ordered data with a metric will be considered in the next section. In Section 2.3, an attempt will be made to generalize the analysis to unordered data but with some means of determining similarity (multidimensional scaling). This will be extended in Section 5.5 to the case in which external information is available about similarity.

2.2 Metric Data

Metric data will have labels or outcomes corresponding to numbers. For example, in the Poisson model of Chapter 1, the labels were the counts of the numbers of suicides in towns of a fixed size in a given year, *i.e.* 0,1,2,... and in the case of the measurement of temperature, the labels were the temperatures recorded, *i.e.* ...,18.3, 18.4,....

As a concrete example, consider the measurement of hours of work missed by employees in a factory over a period of one year, excluding zero time lost (which should be included in the analysis, but which raises separate problems). Suppose that the time lost is recorded to the tenth of an hour. It will rarely happen that two employees miss exactly the same amount of time to the tenth of an hour. The observed frequency distribution might be of the form illustrated in Fig. 2.1. (This is an extreme and unrealistic example, but it illustrates the concept well.) Here, n_1 = 1 employee missed 0.1 hours, n_2 = 1 employee missed 0.3 hours, n_3 = 3 employees each missed 0.4 hours etc. As the number of hours missed increases, many of the possible outcomes (*e.g.* 100.2, 100.3, 100.4, etc.) are not observed and the remaining ones have a single count, n_k = 1 (*e.g.* for 100.1, 100.9, etc.). The sociologist wishes to group the data in order to determine the form of the probability distribution with minimal loss of information. The resulting distribution might be similar to that of Fig. 2.2. Here,

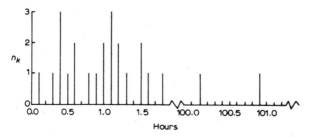

Fig. 2.1 A fictitious example showing the form of the frequency distribution of numbers (n_k) of employees missing work, as measured to 0.1 hours.

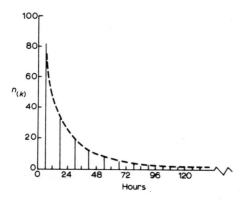

Fig. 2.2. The form of the frequency distribution for fictitious data giving the numbers $(n_{(k)})$ of employees missing work as measured to 0.1 hours but grouped into intervals of 12 hours.

81 employees missed between 0.1 and 12.0 hours of work, 32 between 12.1 and 24.0, etc. The dotted line illustrates the sort of smooth relationship sought among the proportions. If the original outcomes are not grouped under sufficiently few new labels, the form of the distribution will not be evident. If, on the other hand, too few new labels are used, the form of the distribution will be distorted or lost.

In order to avoid confusion, call the original division of observations outcomes, *i.e.* the time missed in tenths of hours, and the new division labels, *e.g.* the time missed in twelve hour periods.

Now assume that the underlying population from which the sample is taken has a frequency distribution with probabilities of possible outcomes varying smoothly as illustrated in Fig. 2.2. To formalize this concept, let $f(y_k)$ be some unknown smooth function describing the change in size of the probability p_k with the

30

outcome y_k, in this example, the time lost (*e.g.* $y_1 = 0.1$, $y_2 = 0.3$, etc. in Fig. 2.1). In addition, let Δy_k be the unit of measurement of the outcome y_k, *i.e.* the amount separating y_k from its neighbours in the population, whether observed in the sample or not. In Fig. 2.1, $\Delta y_k = 0.1$ hours for all values of k. Represent the probability of outcome k by

$$p_k = f(y_k)\Delta y_k \tag{2.1}$$

This formulation may be extended directly to the data grouped under new labels. Suppose that the new labels are renumbered $(k) = (1),(2),...,(K)$ with observed counts for (K) of the labels, $(K) < K$. The smooth function $f(y)$ will remain virtually unchanged after grouping. The new labels, $y_{(k)}$, will be given to the mid-value of the outcomes y_k grouped under the label. For example, in Fig. 2.2, $y_{(1)} = 6.0$ represents the outcomes y_k between 0.1 and 12.0 hours grouped under the first new label. And the new units of measurement will be $\Delta y_{(k)}$, *e.g.* $\Delta y_{(k)} = 12.0$ for all values of (k) in this example. Finally, the probability of an outcome being contained under label $y_{(k)}$ will be $p_{(k)}$ and this will be defined by the same relationship (2.1) with (k) replacing k.

Consider the relationship defined by eqn. (2.1) in the overall population, *i.e.* the true values of p_k and of $f(y_k)$. Suppose that two successive values of p_k are $p_{10} = 0.045$ and $p_{11} = 0.040$ and that the unit of measurement is $y_{10} = y_{11} = 0.1$. Then, $f(y_{10}) = 0.45$ and $f(y_{11}) = 0.40$. This may be represented in Fig. 2.3. The area of each rectangle represents the probability, p_k, of an outcome y_k and the dotted line represents the relationship $f(y_k)$

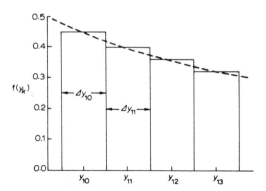

Fig. 2.3 The form of a fictitious probability distribution for the population when the probabilities are related by a smooth function, $f(y_k)$ (broken line), where $p_{10} = 0.045$, $p_{11} = 0.040$ and $\Delta y_{10} = \Delta y_{11} = 0.1$.

31

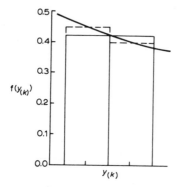

Fig. 2.4 Combination of the probabilities $p_{10} + p_{11} = p_{(k)}$ from Fig. 2.3 when the two labels y_{10} and y_{11} are grouped.

among these probabilities. Now suppose that the outcomes y_{10} and y_{11} are combined under the new label $y_{(k)}$. The probability of observing an individual with label $y_{(k)}$ will be $p_{10} + p_{11} = p_{(k)}$ as represented in Fig. 2.4. Thus,

$$p_{(k)} = f(y_{(k)})(\Delta y_{10} + \Delta y_{11}) = f(y_{(k)})\Delta y_{(k)}$$

to a first approximation. Here, $p_{(k)} = 0.095$ and $\Delta y_{(k)} = 0.2$ giving $f(y_{(k)}) = 0.425$.

For a given sample, eqn. (2.1) may be substituted into the multinomial probability distribution (1.2).

$$\prod_k p_k{}^{n_k} = \prod_k [f(y_k)\Delta y_k]^{n_k}$$

ignoring the factorial coefficient which is not a function of p_k. The logarithm of this equation makes the relationship clearer.

$$\sum_k n_k \log p_k = \sum_k n_k \log f(y_k) + \sum_k n_k \log \Delta y_k \qquad (2.2)$$

If the parameters p_k are replaced by their maximum likelihood estimates of Section 1.3, $\hat{p}_k = n_k/n$, for the given sample from the population, both $\Sigma n_k \log \hat{p}_k$ and $\Sigma n_k \log \Delta y_k$ are known. The remaining term, $\Sigma n_k \log f(y_k)$ is unknown and, for the present discussion, undeterminable.

With $n = 50$, suppose that $n_{10} = 2$, $n_{11} = 1$ and consider the various terms of eqn. (2.2) when the two outcomes are combined. Then, $\hat{p}_{10} = 0.04$, $\hat{p}_{11} = 0.02$, and $\hat{p}_{(k)} = 0.06$. For $\Sigma n_k \log \hat{p}_k$

$$2 \log 0.04 + \log 0.02 = -10.35$$

32

becomes

$3 \log 0.06 = -8.43$

For $\Sigma n_k \log \Delta y_k$

$2 \log 0.1 + \log 0.1 = -6.90$

becomes

$3 \log 0.2 = -4.83$

And for $\Sigma n_k \log f(y_k)$, supposing that the true values are $f(y_{10}) = 0.4$, $f(y_{11}) = 0.2$

$2 \log 0.4 + \log 0.2 = -3.44$

becomes

$3 \log 0.3 = -3.61$.

Thus, the term $\Sigma n_k \log f(y_k)$ remains approximately constant in eqn. (2.2) as the counts for various outcomes are combined if the relationship among the observed proportions is relatively smooth and may be represented by the unknown function $f(y_k)$. And the increase in the size of $\Sigma n_k \log \hat{p}_k$ with grouping is approximately equal to that of $\Sigma n_k \log \Delta y_k$.

This description of the function in eqn. (2.2) is applicable when the outcomes have been combined under labels with sufficiently wide intervals around them ($\Delta y_{(k)}$, the unit of measurement) so that the change from one observed proportion $\hat{p}_k$ to the next is reasonably smooth, as illustrated in Fig. 2.2. Then, $\Sigma n_k \log \hat{p}_k$ and $\Sigma n_k \log \Delta y_k$ increase proportionally as outcomes are combined and eqn. (2.2) describes a straight line with slope one (a 45° line) which cuts the vertical axis at the unknown point $\Sigma n_k \log f(y_k)$.

Consider now the performance of eqn. (2.2) when the observed proportions do not describe a reasonably smooth curve. As a typical combination, suppose that $n_{10} = 1$ and $n_{11} = 0$ so that $\hat{p}_{10} = 0.02$, $\hat{p}_{11} = 0.00$. (This is a slight deviation from the notation previously used, where n_k signified only non-zero counts, but when combining outcomes, all possible intermediate outcomes must be considered for the given unit of measurement, not just those observed.) For $\Sigma n_k \log \hat{p}_k$

$1 \log 0.02 + 0 \log 0.00$

remains unchanged; for $\Sigma n_k \log \Delta y_k$

$1 \log 0.1 + 0 \log 0.1 = -230$

becomes

$1 \log 0.2 = -1.61$

and for $\Sigma n_k \log f(y_k)$

$1 \log f(y_{10}) + 0 \log f(y_{11})$

becomes

$1 \log f(y_{(k)})$

Again, $\Sigma n_k \log f(y_k)$ remains approximately constant but the change in $\Sigma n_k \log \hat{p}_k$ (which will usually be non-zero when all K outcomes are considered) does not correspond to the change in $\Sigma n_k \log \Delta y_k$. Thus, when the observed proportions $\hat{p}_k$ do not describe a smooth relationship $f(y_k)$, as illustrated in Fig. 2.1, eqn. (2.2) will not represent a straight line with slope one.

This equation may be rewritten as

$$\sum_{(k)} n_{(k)} \log (n_{(k)}/n.) = C + \sum_{(k)} n_{(k)} \log \Delta y_{(k)} \qquad (2.3)$$

where only the constant C is unknown. For each set of labels, with the observed outcomes combined to a greater or lesser extent, the values $\Sigma n_{(k)} \log (n_{(k)}/n.)$ and $\Sigma n_{(k)} \log \Delta y_{(k)}$ may be plotted, *using equal sized units on both coordinates.* The resulting graph will be S-shaped, as illustrated in Fig. 2.5, and the region of the curve which follows a straight line with slope one gives the different sets of interval widths $\Delta y_{(k)}$ which are acceptable. Since the

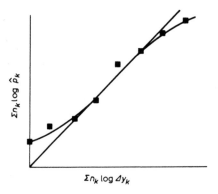

Fig. 2.5 An example of the general form of the graph plotted to determine minimum and maximum interval widths for grouping. The straight line with slope one is placed by eye.

constant C which incorporates the unknown smooth function $f(y_{(k)})$ is unknown, the straight line must be placed by eye, insuring that it has slope one. This method is an approximate graphical procedure, but with a statistical basis for its use (see Lindsey, 1973).

Points on the lower region of the curve which do not follow the straight line correspond to labellings with too few observed counts per label so that the observed $\hat{p}_{(k)}$'s do not follow a smooth curve. Points in the upper region of the curve which do not follow the straight line correspond to combinations of outcomes with too few labels so that the smooth form of the relationship among observed $\hat{p}_{(k)}$'s is distorted or lost. If the sociologist seeks a grouping of the observed counts such that the underlying smooth function $f(y)$ is visible with minimal loss of information about counts of outcomes as originally observed, a labelling as low on the curve as possible which still lies on the straight line will be selected. Conversely, if he seeks a minimum number of labels having observed counts without distorting or losing the underlying distribution, a labelling as high as possible on the curve still lying on the straight line will be selected. In either case, sufficient arbitrariness remains to allow choice of a meaningful set of groups.

Let us now reconsider the example of hours of work missed in a factory using the set of numerical data (generated by a computer)

TABLE 2.1

Numbers $(n_{(k)})$ of workers in a sample of 185 missing various periods of work, as measured to 0.1 hours and grouped into intervals of 6.4 hours. Computer generated data.

Interval	$n_{(k)}$	Interval	$n_{(k)}$	Interval	$n_{(k)}$
0.1— 6.4	57	89.7— 96.0	6	294.5—300.8	1
6.5—12.8	24	96.1—102.4	1	332.9—339.2	1
12.9—19.2	10	102.5—108.8	1	390.5—396.8	1
19.3—25.6	8	108.9—115.2	2	422.5—428.8	1
25.7—32.0	8	115.3—121.6	1	428.9—435.2	1
32.1—38.4	10	128.1—134.4	1	435.3—441.6	2
38.5—44.8	10	147.3—153.6	1	441.7—448.0	1
44.9—51.2	6	185.7—192.0	1	473.7—480.0	1
51.3—57.6	4	192.1—198.4	1	486.5—492.8	2
57.7—64.0	5	204.9—211.2	1	499.3—505.6	1
64.1—70.4	3	224.1—230.4	1	889.7—896.0	1
70.5—76.8	4	249.7—256.0	1	966.5—972.8	1
83.2—89.6	4				

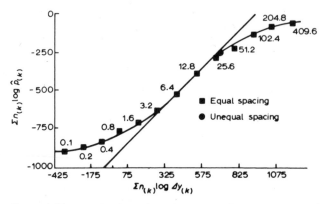

Fig. 2.6 The graph plotted to determine the maximum and minimum interval widths for grouping the data ($n = 185$) on hours of work missed given in Table 2.1. The sizes of the intervals with equal spacing are marked on the graph. The one grouping with unequal spacing has the first four intervals 24.0 hours and the rest 96.0 hours.

given in Table 2.1. For economy of space, the partially grouped data have been given instead of the original observations. A convenient procedure for constructing the curve of Fig. 2.5 for data such as these is to combine adjacent outcomes in pairs, so that $\Delta y_k = 0.1$ and $\Delta y_{(k)} = 0.2, 0.4, 0.8$, etc. for all values of (k) until a very few groups remain. The intervals given in Table 2.1 are for the sixth successive labelling, with $\Delta y_{(k)} = 6.4$ hours for all values of (k). From the plot, the general shape of the curve may be determined and the straight line with slope one placed. This has been done in Fig. 2.6, where the interval widths, Δy, are marked beside the corresponding points.

From inspection of the curve of Fig. 2.6, a useful grouping interval appears to fall in the region between 7 and 24 hours. If the sociologist is interested in determining the relationship among the probabilities of an employee missing various amounts of work, he may consider grouping the data into days (of 8 hours) lost in the year. This interval size will permit him to discern the shape of the probability distribution with minimal loss of information. The first interval (label) will contain the number of employees losing one day (8 hours) or less of work (not including those missing no time, these not being included in the sample), the second between 8.1 and 16 hours (*i.e.* between one and two days), and so on.

On the other hand, if the sociologist is interested in reducing the data to contain as few intervals as possible, he may chose interval widths of 3 days (in the same way as for one day, the first interval contains the count for those missing 0.1 to 24 hours, etc.). Since the distribution has an extremely long tail, one may wish to combine the few counts found there into a smaller number of intervals. For example, the first four intervals might be of 3 days each ($\Delta y_{(1)} = \Delta y_{(2)} = \Delta y_{(3)} = \Delta y_{(4)} = 24.0$) and then succeeding intervals of 12 days each ($\Delta y_{(k)} = 96.0$ for $(k) > 4$). Again, the two terms of eqn. (2.3) may be calculated and the point marked on the graph (the circle in Fig. 2.6). If this point appears to fall on (or lie very close to) the straight line with slope one, the grouping should be acceptable. If it does not, the shape of the frequency distribution has been distorted by the larger interval widths. Note that the point must lie on the straight line and not just on the S curve formed by points previously plotted. When intervals in the tail are combined in this manner, the point plotted will lie slightly higher than the corresponding point with constant interval widths (in this case, a point with $\Delta y_{(k)} = 24.0$ for all values of (k), lying near that for 25.6).

The procedure described in this section requires observations on a considerable number of individuals in order to be useful. The minimum number will depend on the dispersion of the data and on the number of intervals desired (more observations for more intervals). For example, the dispersion of the data of Table 2.1 is relatively great due to the very long tail. For data with smaller dispersion, such as that thought to follow a normal distribution, 50 to 100 observations may be sufficient. In the above example, $n = 185$ was barely enough, since the S curve follows the straight line over a very small region.

Consider, now, the analysis of the same type of data but with the number of observations increased approximately twelve times so that $n = 2213$. In all respects, the data are the same as previously, but they have been given in more detail in Table 2.2, the counts being combined into intervals $\Delta y_{(k)} = 1.2$ hours instead of the intervals of 6.4 hours in Table 2.1. As before, the original, uncombined (computer generated) data were measured to 0.1 hours of work missed.

As in the previous example, points from eqn. (2.3), as the constant interval width is doubled from 0.1 to 0.2, 0.4, 0.8, etc., are plotted in Fig. 2.7, producing the S curve of the graph. With these data, the straight line with slope one may be easily placed since the S curve follows a straight line over a much larger region than in Fig. 2.6. The possible grouping intervals range from about one

TABLE 2.2

Numbers ($n_{(k)}$) of workers in a sample of 2213 missing various periods of work measured to 0.1 hours and grouped in intervals of 1.2 hours. Computer generated data.

Interval	$n_{(k)}$	Interval	$n_{(k)}$	Interval	$n_{(k)}$
0.1— 1.2	138	42.1—43.2	14	85.3— 86.4	6
1.3— 2.4	222	43.3—44.4	11	86.5— 87.6	3
2.5— 3.6	138	44.5—45.6	11	87.7— 88.8	6
3.7— 4.8	141	45.7—46.8	15	88.9— 90.0	11
4.9— 6.0	112	46.9—48.0	13	90.1— 91.2	11
6.1— 7.2	106	48.1—49.2	10	91.3— 92.4	6
7.3— 8.4	96	49.3—50.4	5	92.5— 93.6	5
8.5— 9.6	66	50.5—51.6	7	93.7— 94.8	12
9.7—10.8	46	51.7—52.8	7	94.9— 96.0	7
10.9—12.0	56	52.9—54.0	6	96.1— 97.2	8
12.1—13.2	41	54.1—55.2	1	97.3— 98.4	9
13.3—14.4	36	55.3—56.4	7	98.5— 99.6	2
14.5—15.6	29	56.5—57.6	7	99.7—100.8	1
15.7—16.8	30	57.7—58.8	9	100.9—102.0	4
16.9—18.0	32	58.9—60.0	4	102.1—103.2	5
18.1—19.2	22	60.1—61.2	4	103.3—104.4	5
19.3—20.4	26	61.3—62.4	7	104.5—105.6	9
20.5—21.6	22	62.5—63.6	6	105.7—106.8	6
21.7—22.8	26	63.7—64.8	5	106.9—108.0	4
22.9—24.0	25	64.9—66.0	3	108.1—109.2	1
24.1—25.2	10	66.1—67.2	6	109.3—110.4	1
25.3—26.4	18	67.3—68.4	4	110.5—111.6	5
26.5—27.6	22	68.5—69.6	5	111.7—112.8	1
27.7—28.8	24	69.7—70.8	5	114.1—115.2	5
28.9—30.0	15	70.9—72.0	4	115.3—116.4	3
30.1—31.2	16	72.1—73.2	3	116.5—117.6	2
31.3—32.4	17	73.3—74.4	2	117.7—118.8	2
32.5—33.6	18	74.5—75.6	4	118.9—120.0	2
33.7—34.8	16	75.7—76.8	5	122.5—123.6	3
34.9—36.0	5	76.9—78.0	2	123.7—124.8	3
36.1—37.2	8	79.3—80.4	3	124.9—126.0	1
37.3—38.4	10	80.5—81.6	6	126.1—127.2	7
38.5—39.6	12	81.7—82.8	6	127.3—128.4	5
39.7—40.8	18	82.9—84.0	9	128.5—129.6	1
40.9—42.0	15	84.1—85.2	2	⩾129.7	201

hour to about 24 hours. If the sociologist wishes to determine the shape of the frequency distribution of hours of work missed in the year, he may choose the much finer labelling of the counts at intervals of one hour for this larger set of data as compared with

38

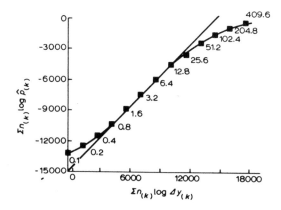

Fig. 2.7 The graph plotted to determine the maximum and minimum interval widths for grouping the data ($n_. = 2213$) on hours of work missed given in Table 2.2. Comparison with Fig. 2.6 shows the increased range of acceptable interval widths with increased sample size.

the eight hour (one day) intervals of the previous set of data. This is a logical result since the procedure is intended to eliminate the random fluctuation of observed counts among adjacent possible outcomes, as illustrated by the difference between Fig. 2.1 and 2.2, by grouping the outcomes so that a sufficient number of counts are observed for each label. If many more counts are available, a larger number of labels may be used and the shape of the probability distribution may be determined more accurately.

At the other extreme, the maximum amount of grouping without distorting the frequency distribution remains about the same, with three-day intervals. In fact, a two-day interval seems to be nearer the maximum in Fig. 2.7. From Table 2.2, one may see that larger intervals would combine the high counts in the range 0.1— 12.0 with the much smaller counts following, in this way distorting the shape of the distribution. Since the position of the straight line in Fig. 2.6 is not as clearly defined, a maximum interval width of about two days (16 hours) for that set of data (Table 2.1) should also be used.

In applying this procedure, two points should be kept in mind. This is an approximate procedure, both in the use of eqn. (2.1) which is a numerical approximation to a probability function and in the placing of the straight line with slope one which must be done by eye. Both of these approximations become more exact as the number of observations is increased, as illustrated by the dif-

39

ference between Figs. 2.6 and 2.7. Also, care must be taken in placing the straight line, especially if the scales of the two coordinates are not the same since, in this case, a line with slope one will not lie at 45° to the axes. In each of the plots given, the two scales have been made the same.

In the discussion so far in this section, the labelling of the counts has been assumed continuous, as defined in Section 1.1. The generalization to a discrete ordered labelling with metric is straightforward. The counts of suicides in various towns given in Chapter 1 is an example of this form of labelling, although that specific type of data would not usually require grouping.

Consider the numbers of pupils attending primary school in a given country and count the number of schools of each size in a random sample. Then, n_k will be the number of schools with k pupils. In this case, the interval between outcomes is $\Delta y_k = 1$ pupil and k may range from one to, say, 1000 or more with probability p_k of observing a school with k pupils. The data in this form have limited use; the sociologist will want to group the counts under labels corresponding to schools with various numbers of students. The problem is identical to that previously treated, having two possibilities depending on whether the sociologist seeks a maximum or a minimum number of labels.

The sizes of 80 such schools (adapted from biological data of Bliss (1967)) are given in Table 2.3. Most school sizes appear only once in the table. When more than one school is observed with the same number of pupils, the number of schools is given in parentheses. Since schools similar in other respects have been chosen, the range in size is not great. The two terms of eqn. (2.3) are plotted in Fig. 2.8 to determine possible groupings of the school sizes.

TABLE 2.3

Numbers of pupils attending 80 different schools. When several schools have the same number of pupils, the number of such schools is given in parentheses. Adapted from biological data of Bliss (1967, p.122).

210	235	251	259	273	283(2)	291	299	314
215(2)	236	253	260(3)	274	284	292	300	319
218	240(2)	254(2)	261	275(3)	285(3)	293(2)	302	330
226	241(2)	255	267(3)	279	286(2)	294	307	339
228	243	256	270	280(4)	287	296	309	345
230	244	258(2)	271(3)	282	289	298(2)	310(2)	366
233(2)	248							

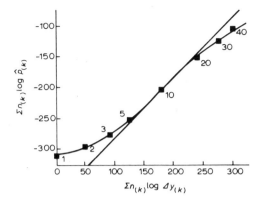

Fig. 2.8 The graph plotted to determine the maximum and minimum interval widths for grouping the data on numbers of pupils in schools given in Table 2.3.

The range of possible interval widths lies between a difference in school size of about 7 and 20 pupils. Consider in turn the two extremes. Suppose that the sociologist wishes to determine the underlying probability distribution of the population of similar schools with minimal loss of information about the actual size of individual schools. Perhaps a value of $\Delta y_{(k)} = 7$ will be chosen. The observed frequency distribution for this labelling is given in Fig. 2.9. The median or centre value of each set of outcomes is given on the graph, i.e. 210 represents those schools with between 207 and 213 pupils, with one such school observed, etc. A smooth curve has been sketched relating the values of $\hat{p}_{(k)}$. Mathematical description of such curves will be briefly discussed in Section 2.4. As can be seen from the figure, fluctuations in $\hat{p}_{(k)}$ still exist, such as that for the interval 263 to 269 pupils, but these are probably due to the small sample size since the overall shape of the distribution is discernable.

Suppose now that the sociologist is interested in obtaining the maximum possible condensation of the data without distorting the form of the frequency distribution. The interval $\Delta y_{(k)} = 20$ may be chosen yielding the frequency distribution given in Fig. 2.10. Here, the label 215 signifies schools with numbers of pupils ranging from 205 to 224, etc. Although different scales have been used, Figs. 2.9 and 2.10 may be seen to show the same form of frequency distribution.

In the construction of these two figures, the choice of the point from which to start taking labels is arbitrary. For example, in

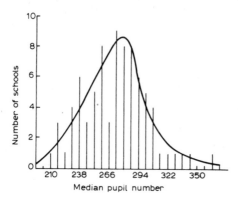

Fig. 2.9 The frequency distribution for the numbers of schools having different numbers of pupils given in Table 2.3 when the data are grouped into equal sized intervals of seven pupils, the minimum width determined from Fig. 2.8.

Fig. 2.9, the first interval starts at 207 pupils and in Fig. 2.10 at 205. This choice should be made as objectively or randomly as possible, but any reasonable choice should yield virtually the same results. If not, the data should be checked for errors, especially in recording. For example, a person may unconsciously prefer even to odd numbers or numbers ending in zero to those ending in 9 or 1 and thus make several similar mistakes in recording the numbers.

The frequency distribution derived by this method may some-

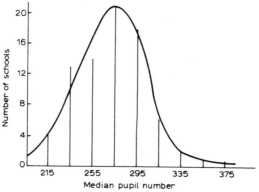

Fig. 2.10 The frequency distribution for the numbers of schools having different numbers of pupils given in Table 2.3, when the data are grouped into equal sized intervals of twenty pupils, the maximum width determined from Fig. 2.8. Comparison may be made with Fig. 2.9.

42

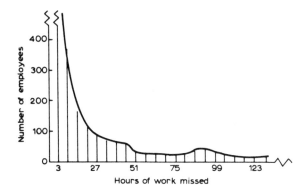

Fig. 2.11 The frequency distribution of the hours of work missed by 2213 employees given in Table 2.2 using an interval width of six hours. The count for 0.0—6.0 hours is 751 employees.

times not appear to follow a simple curve as sought. Although a smooth curve, it may not have a simple form such as those of Figs. 2.2, 2.9, and 2.10. Consider, for example, the data of Table 2.2. After relatively small numbers of men missing from, say, 8 to 10 days (64 to 80 hours) work, the counts increase again in the region of 11 and 12 days (88 to 98 hours) missed. With a grouping of 6 hour intervals, these data have been plotted as the frequency distribution of Fig. 2.11. Here the increase for the interval 90.1 to 96.0 hours can be seen. Further investigation may be important to determine if any underlying causes for this increase exist. If such causes are found, the sample of individuals should not, in fact, be considered homogeneous but should be split into two or more groups according to the causes determined. In other words, factors which were originally assumed not to affect various individuals differently with respect to work missed must now be accounted for. The analysis may be continued using the procedures to be described in Chapters 3 and 4 for differences among groups.

Note that the fluctuations in Fig. 2.11 are worth considering because the counts for the corresponding labels are large ($n_{(k)}$ = 41 for the interval 90.1 to 96.0 hours) whereas in Fig. 2.9, they are very small ($n_{(k)}$ = 3 for the interval 263 to 269 pupils). Fluctuations further out in the tail of Fig. 2.11, where the counts are also very small, may have little significance.

43

2.3 Ordinal and Multidimensional Data

The problem of combining outcomes becomes much more difficult and ill-defined when ordinal or unordered data, which cannot
be placed on a unidimensional ranking scale, are considered. The
final labelling depends, to a large extent, on the specific reason for
reducing the number of observed outcomes (or of parameters, p_k).
The procedure cannot be well-defined statistically as it could in
Section 2.2. Any method of combining outcomes will depend arbitrarily on how similarity among the outcomes is defined and this
in turn will depend on the reason for reducing the number of
different outcomes.

Consider, for example, a large number of individuals classified
according to occupation, which the sociologist wishes to group
into a smaller number of categories. Some of the occupations will
be very similar to others in the sample according to some criterion
of interest to the sociologist (socio-economic status, work environ-
ment, amount of education required, etc.) while others will be
unrelated to the rest. By some criterion, store clerk and service
station attendant might be similar and farmer much different.

In order to begin to construct the graph of Fig. 2.5, each occupation is assumed to be assigned an interval $\Delta y = 1$. The data are
inspected to determine those occupations which are most similar.
Each set of occupations (2 or 3 each) with the greatest degree of
similarity is given a new label, (k). All occupations more different
than this greatest degree are left separate. Each of these sets or
single occupations may be said to have interval $\Delta y_{(k)} = 2$. Again,
the greatest remaining degree of similarity is determined, the combinations made, and new labels assigned. At this stage, some of the
previous sets may be combined, some separate occupations combined with the sets or among themselves to form a new set and
some remain separate. Then, each set or single occupation has
interval $\Delta y_{(k)} = 4$. This process may be continued until all occupations have been combined under a few labels. The two terms of
eqn. (2.3) are calculated at each stage and these points plotted on
a graph. An appropriate grouping is chosen in the same way as in
Section 2.2.

The interval Δy in the above discussion may be interpreted, for
example when $\Delta y = 1$, as meaning that at least one unit of difference exists between each occupation and the next most similar
and, with many, much more; when $\Delta y = 2$, that all occupations
with not more than two units of difference have been combined

44

into sets; etc. This procedure assumes only a distance (similarity-difference) among adjacent occupations or sets of occupations and not a linear ordering as was used in Section 2.2. Hence, the assumptions of the procedure have been weakened, but with accompanying loss of objective means of implementing the method. In addition, since supplementary information for measuring similarity, such as income level, etc., will usually be available, in which case the method of Section 5.5 will be applied, the procedure of this section is of extremely limited usefulness.

The grouping of ordinal data, with no available metric, is usually equally arbitrary. For example, if the data concern educational level, the years of education are usually grouped into primary, secondary, and post-secondary. In general, grouping of ordinal data may also be attacked in the same way as a multidimensional scaling problem as discussed above and in Section 5.5.

2.4 Relationships among Responses

From the preceding discussion, the reader may wonder what relation the function $f(y_k)$ of eqn. (2.1) has to the basic analyses of Chapter 1. He may have noted that this function provides a relationship among the probabilities p_k of observing various outcomes in the same way as does eqn. (1.4). Indeed, these two equations are equivalent

$$p_k = p_k(\theta_1,...,\theta_G) = f(y_k)\Delta y_k \qquad (k = 1,...,K) \qquad (2.4)$$

Only the idea expressed is different. With $p_k(\theta_1,...,\theta_G)$, the fact that the unknown parameters, $\theta_1,...,\theta_G$, describe the relation among the probabilities, p_k, is emphasized. The labelling, y_k, is incorporated into the function $p_k(\cdot)$. With $f(y_k)$, the change in the probability, p_k, with change in label, y_k, and the unit of measurement, Δy_k, are emphasized and the unknown parameters, θ_g, are included in the function $f(\cdot)$. Equation (2.4) may be rewritten as

$$p_k = f(y_k;\theta_1,...,\theta_G)\Delta y_k \qquad (k = 1, ..., K) \qquad (2.5)$$

using the features of the two representations.

In Chapter 1, the Poisson probability distribution was used as an illustration of this relationship. In that example, a group of towns was examined and the number of suicides in each in a year determined. The number of towns with each number of suicides is counted; the label is the number of suicides committed each year in the town, $y_k = k$ ($k=0,1,...$), and the unknown parameter, θ, is the average number of suicides in the population of towns from which the group was sampled. Equation (1.5) describes this relationship among the probabilities, p_k, of observing the labels, y_k, for a given value of the parameter θ. Of course, one factor in eqn. (2.5) still remains: Δy_k, the interval about the label y_k or the unit of measurement. Since a fraction of a suicide cannot be observed, the unit is $\Delta y_k = 1$ (all k). Equation (1.5) may be rewritten as

$$p_k = \frac{\theta^{y_k} e^{-\theta}}{y_k!} \Delta y_k \qquad (\Delta y_k = 1; y_k = k = 0,1,...) \qquad (2.6)$$

where

$$f(y_k;\theta) = \frac{\theta^{y_k} e^{-\theta}}{y_k!}$$

Since the Poisson distribution is used to describe rare or random events, the sociologist will rarely encounter data generated by this process which need grouping using the procedures of Section 2.2. In other words, non-zero counts, n_k, for a large number of different labels, y_k, will not usually be observed.

Equation (2.5) expresses a relationship among four quantities: the label, y_k, describing an observation on an individual; the precision, Δy_k, with which the observation has been made; an unknown set of parameters, $\theta_1,..., \theta_G$, describing a relationship among the labels for the overall population; and the probability, p_k, of observing the given label rather than any other, this also being the frequency with which the label occurs in the overall population. Although this book is concerned primarily with the counts of the numbers of times the various labels are observed in a sample, as expressed by $\hat{p}_k$, and not with the role of the labels themselves, some further discussion of the treatment of the label, y_k, and its parameters, $\theta_1,..., \theta_G$, may be worthwhile.

A large body of the theory of statistics is concerned with discovering what one may learn about the labels observed in a sample of individuals. In such cases, the sample within a homogeneous group may be very small, even one or two individuals in some problems of the type considered in Chapters 3 and 4. Then, the counts provide virtually no information and a frequency distribution cannot really be said to have been observed. Virtually all of the information resides in the label observed. With such samples, two different situations may exist *a priori*: one may or may not be able to assume from previous more extensive, sampling or from theoretical considerations that the observations should follow some well-defined probability distribution. If so, this distribution is used in the analysis, although the sample at hand provides virtually no means of verifying the assumption. If not, a normal distribution is adopted because of various nice theoretical properties and because it is well documented and familiar, but again with little means of verification for the observed sample.

When a large number of individuals has been sampled, as has been considered until now in this chapter, the normal distribution may be considered as a possible candidate for the function $f(y_k; \theta_1,...,\theta_G)$ of eqn. (2.5). The first assumption which the normal distribution makes is that the labelling is a continuous variable which may take any value between plus and minus infinity. But, as pointed out in Section 1.2, the infinite range of y_k does not create serious problems in using eqn. (2.5) since most of the probabilities, p_k, in the multinomial likelihood function (1.7) will be virtually zero and those corresponding to unobserved labels ($n_k = 0$) in the sample will disappear. The assumption of a continuous variable is a mathematical convenience representing the concept that the label can have any value in the permissible range but only approximating the observable situation in which the label is only measurable within the limits of precision of the measuring device, as defined by Δy_k. Thus, the use of the normal distribution may be extended to data with labels which are, in concept, discrete, such as the number of suicides in a town or the number of pupils in a school, with no greater approximation than is actually the case with continuous variables. But care should be taken if the discrete labels cannot be negative, as with counts, and if the mean of the labels is near zero, as with the suicide example, since the normal distribution will provide relatively large probabilities of negative counts. This will be reflected in the small plausibility found for the normal distribution with such data.

Consider the form which eqn. (2.5) takes for the normal distribution. Since this is a continuous distribution, to determine the probability of the label y_k falling in the interval $y_k - \frac{1}{2}\Delta y_k$, $y_k + \frac{1}{2}\Delta y_k$, one must integrate over this region

$$p_k = \int_{y_k - \frac{1}{2}\Delta y_k}^{y_k + \frac{1}{2}\Delta y_k} \frac{1}{\sqrt{2\pi\theta_2}} \exp[-\frac{1}{2\theta_2}(x - \theta_1)^2]\, dx \qquad (2.7)$$

47

Analysis of this expression shows that the unknown parameter θ_1 expresses the average value of the label y_k in the population and that θ_2 expresses the variance of y_k in the population, *i.e.* a measure of the degree of variation in the values of the label in the population.

Since eqn. (2.7) is a complicated expression, its relation to eqn. (2.5) is not evident. Indeed, eqn. (2.5) does not adequately represent this expression; it should rather be

$$p_k = g(y_k, \Delta y_k; \theta_1, \theta_2)$$

Fortunately, eqn. (2.7) may be simplified by the use of a numerical approximation; this yields

$$p_k \doteq \frac{1}{\sqrt{2\pi\theta_2}} \exp[-\frac{1}{2\theta_2}(y_k - \theta_1)^2] \, \Delta y_k \tag{2.8}$$

This new expression, which is virtually indistinguishable from the first within the limits of numerical accuracy usually encountered (see Kalbfleisch, 1971, Chap. 5), illuminates the application of eqn. (2.5) to the normal distribution. When the procedures of Section 2.2 have been completed, the normal distribution, with values of θ_1, θ_2 to be estimated, is one possible candidate for the unknown function $f(y_k)$ in eqn. (2.1).

This normal probability model may be applied to the data of Table 2.3, after grouping the data with $\Delta y = 7$ as in Fig. 2.9, to determine if it represents a plausible candidate to explain how these data were generated. In order to do this, follow the procedure outlined in Section 1.3 for the Poisson distribution. For this, values of the parameters θ_1 and θ_2 are required. Since these parameters describe the labels, their maximum likelihood estimates must be calculated using the ungrouped data of Table 2.3 so that no information about the labels observed is lost. Equation (2.8) may be substituted into the multinomial relative likelihood function (1.11) to yield

$$R_M(\text{normal with } \theta_1, \theta_2)$$

$$= \prod_k \left\{ \left[\frac{1}{\sqrt{2\pi\theta_2}} \exp[-\frac{1}{2\theta_2}(y_k - \theta_1)^2] \, \Delta y_k \right] \Big/ \hat{p}_k \right\}^{n_k} \tag{2.9}$$

Substitution of the values of y_k, $\Delta y_k (=1)$, and n_k and maximization of the function yields $\hat{\theta}_1 = 272.7$ pupils and $\hat{\theta}_2 = 941.21$. The function, $R_M(\text{normal with } \hat{\theta}_1, \hat{\theta}_2)$ may now be used to compare

48

the most plausible description of the observed data using the normal distribution to the most plausible in general (the multinomial distribution). Since the frequencies of observed labels are being compared, the grouped data $(\Delta y{=}7)$ are now used, yielding the value R_M (normal with $\hat{\theta}_1{=}272.7$, $\hat{\theta}_2{=}941.21$) = $8.2{\times}10^{-5}$. This may appear to indicate a very considerable loss of descriptive power, but consider the situation more closely. Instead of the approximately $(K){-}1{=}22$ parameters corresponding to the labels of Fig. 2.9, with no relationship among them, the normal distribution has 2 parameters with a well-defined relationship among the labels: $\hat{\theta}_1 = \Sigma n_{(k)} y_{(k)}/n$. and $\hat{\theta}_2 = \Sigma n_{(k)} (y_{(k)}{-}\hat{\theta}_1)/n$. But how does the sociologist determine when the value of the relative likelihood is so small that the gain in description of the labels (relationship among counts) is not worth the loss in description of the size of the counts? This is, in many ways, a question which must be answered for the individual set of data by weighing the relative importance of the two factors. A very approximate theoretical relationship does exist between the description of counts and of labels, but it should be used with care. If the total number of parameters in the two probability models to be compared is fixed (which is not so in this case, since $n_{(k)} = 0$ for $y_{(k)} = 350$ and 357 and one might observe individuals with labels 203 or 371 etc. in another similar sample), then $-2 \log R_M$ (normal with $\hat{\theta}_1, \hat{\theta}_2$) has a Chi-squared distribution with degrees of freedom equal to the difference in the number of parameters estimated (in this case, approximately $22{-}2 = 20$) which may be used in a test of significance. For this set of data, $\chi^2_{20} \doteq 18.8$ giving $p \doteq 0.50$. Thus, for this example, the interpretation of the approximation is not difficult even though neither assumption is fulfilled: the normal probability model may be considered plausible.

This analysis does not imply that the data were actually generated by a normal distribution but only that this hypothesis is plausible. If another probability model is found to be even more plausible and if no sociological reasons against it exist, the normal model will be replaced. Indeed, from both Figs. 2.9 and 2.10, the reader may have noticed that the frequency distribution of these data has a longer tail to the right than to the left. Since the normal distribution is symmetric, another model taking this discrepancy into account may be sought. Two of the possible candidates are the log normal and the two-parameter gamma probability models. When the preceding analysis is applied, both of these models are found to be about 2.5 times as plausible (make the data 2.5 times as probable) as the normal model using the same number (2) of parameters. Thus, R_M (log normal or gamma with $\hat{\theta}_1, \hat{\theta}_2$) = 2 × 10^{-4}. Another possible objection to all three of these models is that they assume that the labelling is a continuous variable, whereas y_k is actually a count of pupils in a school. The next step in refining the probability model might be to find a discrete analogue of the log normal or of the gamma distribution.

In this section, the analysis of count data has been abandoned and the field of "label analysis" entered. Hopefully, this has provided the reader with some idea of how the analyses in the rest of the book are related to more traditional statistical procedures, in particular using normal distribution theory.

2.5 Further Aspects of Analysis within a Group

Two other basic problems often arise in the analysis of count data within a homogeneous group of individuals. Two or more sets of data may be available, either samples taken at different locations or at different times or supplementary samples taken to increase the size n of an initial sample. The sociologist wishes to determine if all of the samples might plausibly have arisen from the same population of individuals, so that the sets may be combined. A second problem involves the derivation and determination of plausibility of theoretical values of the probabilities, p_k, of the outcomes for a given sample.

Suppose that, in the example concerning the number of pupils in schools of the previous section, the sociologist takes a further sample, n_2 = 70, of schools with results as given in Table 2.4. From this table and Table 2.3, the estimated probabilities of ob-

TABLE 2.4

Numbers of pupils attending 70 different schools. When several schools have the same number of pupils, the number of such schools is given in parentheses. Adapted from biological data of Bliss (1967, p.106).

203	228	241	254	263	274	283(2)	291	319
212	230	243	255	266(2)	275(2)	284	299	322
215	233	245	256	267(4)	276	285(4)	302	327
218	235	246	258	270(2)	277(2)	286(2)	304	330
222(2)	237	250	259	271	280(2)	287	307	338
226	240(2)	252	260	273	281(2)	289	310	339

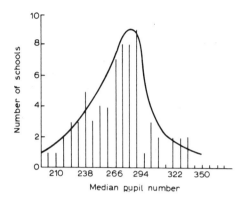

Fig. 2.12 The frequency distribution for the numbers of schools having different numbers of pupils given in Table 2.4, when the data are grouped into minimum equal sized intervals of seven pupils. Comparison may be made with the equivalent distribution for the data of Table 2.3 as given in Fig. 2.9.

serving a given size of school are to be compared. A problem arises since, for example, the probability of 203 pupils, as derived from the second sample is estimated to be $\hat{p}_{203} = 1/70$, using an obvious notation, whereas it is zero from the first. And conversely, $\hat{p}_{210} = 1/80$ from the first and zero from the second sample. This is the case with a large number of the school sizes observed in the two samples. But suppose that the probability of a school having between, say, 200 and 210 pupils, etc. is considered. Then, virtually all of the estimated probabilities will be non-zero and comparable. Thus, the grouping procedure of Section 2.2 must be applied to this sample as well. The plot of the two terms of eqn. (2.3) yields a graph very similar to that of Fig. 2.8 with interval widths in the same range, 7 to 20 pupils. The minimum is chosen in order to reduce the loss of information about the labels and the observed frequency distribution for the sample is plotted in Fig. 2.12. Inspection of this graph reveals no smooth relationship among the observed counts, although it may be somewhat suggestive of the corresponding plot for the first sample given in Fig. 2.9. The variability in the counts may be due to lack of sufficient observations in each of the samples.

Two hypotheses are to be compared as to plausibility: that the two samples come from two populations of schools containing different proportions of the various pupil numbers and that they come from the same population. For the first hypothesis, denote the proportions of school sizes in the first population by $p_{1(k)}$

51

TABLE 2.5

Frequency distribution and estimated probabilities for two samples and the combined sample of numbers of pupils attending schools, grouped into intervals of 7 pupils, as derived from the data of Tables 2.3 and 2.4.

Interval	$n_{1(k)}$	$n_{2(k)}$	$n_{(k)}$	$\hat{p}_{1(k)}$	$\hat{p}_{2(k)}$	$\hat{p}_{(k)}$
200—206	0	1	1	0.0	0.0143	0.0067
207—213	1	1	2	0.0125	0.0143	0.0133
214—220	3	2	5	0.0375	0.0286	0.0333
221—227	1	3	4	0.0125	0.0419	0.0267
228—234	4	3	7	0.0500	0.0419	0.0467
235—241	6	5	11	0.0750	0.0714	0.0733
242—248	3	3	6	0.0375	0.0419	0.0400
249—255	5	4	9	0.0625	0.0571	0.0600
256—262	8	4	12	0.1000	0.0571	0.0800
263—269	3	7	10	0.0375	0.1000	0.0667
270—276	9	8	17	0.1125	0.1142	0.1133
277—283	8	8	16	0.1000	0.1142	0.1067
284—290	8	9	17	0.1000	0.1285	0.1133
291—297	6	1	7	0.0750	0.0143	0.0467
298—304	5	3	8	0.0625	0.0419	0.0533
305—311	4	2	6	0.0500	0.0286	0.0400
312—318	1	0	1	0.0125	0.0	0.0067
319—325	1	2	3	0.0125	0.0286	0.0200
326—332	1	2	3	0.0125	0.0286	0.0200
333—339	1	2	3	0.0125	0.0286	0.0200
340—346	1	0	1	0.0125	0.0	0.0067
347—353	0	0	0	0.0	0.0	0.0
354—360	0	0	0	0.0	0.0	0.0
361—367	1	0	1	0.0125	0.0	0.0067

(the $p_{(k)}$ of Section 2.2) and in the second by $p_{2(k)}$. For the second hypothesis, denote the proportions by $p_{(k)}$. Since the two samples are assumed to be observed independently, the probability of observing the two samples given some fixed values of the $p_{1(k)}$'s and $p_{2(k)}$'s is the product of the probabilities of observing each sample. Thus, the likelihood function is the product of the two corresponding multinomial likelihood functions:

$$L_{M_1M_2}(p_{1(k)}, p_{2(k)}, (k)=(1),...,(K)) = C \prod_k p_{1(k)}^{n_{1(k)}} p_{2(k)}^{n_{2(k)}} \qquad (2.10)$$

where (K) is the total number of different grouped school sizes observed in the two samples. Under the second hypothesis, since the two samples are considered to come from the same popula-

52

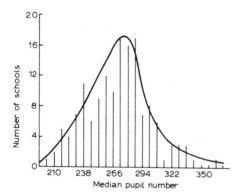

Fig. 2.13 The frequency distribution for the numbers of schools having different numbers of pupils for the samples of Tables 2.3 and 2.4 combined when the data are grouped into equal sized intervals of seven pupils. Comparison may be made with the distributions for the individual samples, Figs. 2.9 and 2.12.

tion, the samples are combined, and the multinomial likelihood function (1.7) used

$$L_M(p_{(k)}, (k)=(1),...,(K)) = C \prod_k p_{(k)}^{n_{1(k)}+n_{2(k)}} \tag{2.11}$$

The maximum likelihood estimates of the parameters are $\hat{p}_{1(k)} = n_{1(k)}/n_{1.}$, $\hat{p}_{2(k)} = n_{2(k)}/n_{2.}$, and $\hat{p}_{(k)} = (n_{1(k)} + n_{2(k)})/(n_{1.} + n_{2.})$. These results are summarized in Table 2.5. Notice from this tabulation that $\hat{p}_{(k)}$ is not the average of $\hat{p}_{1(k)}$ and $\hat{p}_{2(k)}$ but that it is automatically weighted for difference in sample size, $n_{1.} = 80$, $n_{2.} = 70$. The corresponding frequency distribution for the combined data is given in Fig. 2.13.

Compare now the relative plausibility of the two hypotheses, *i.e.* the maximum probability of observing the data from the samples under the two hypotheses. The maximum likelihood estimates of the three sets of parameters may be substituted into eqns. (2.10) and (2.11) and their ratio determined

$$R_{M_1M_2}(\text{data combined with } \hat{p}_{(k)}) = \prod_k \left[\frac{\hat{p}_{(k)}}{\hat{p}_{1(k)}}\right]^{n_{1(k)}} \left[\frac{\hat{p}_{(k)}}{\hat{p}_{2(k)}}\right]^{n_{2(k)}} \tag{2.12}$$

This is equivalent to forming the relative likelihood ratio (analogous to eqn. (1.11)) from eqn. (2.10)

53

$$R_{M_1M_2}(p_{1(k)}, p_{2(k)}) = \prod_k \left[\frac{p_{1(k)}}{\hat{p}_{1(k)}}\right]^{n_{1(k)}} \left[\frac{p_{2(k)}}{\hat{p}_{2(k)}}\right]^{n_{2(k)}}$$

and then considering $R_{M_1M_2}(p_{1(k)} = p_{2(k)} = \hat{p}_{(k)})$. These calculations yield the value $R_{M_1M_2}(p_{1(k)} = p_{2(k)} = \hat{p}_{(k)}) = 3.8 \times 10^{-4}$. The same remarks apply to this value as to the value obtained in the previous section for the representation of the first sample by a normal distribution. The number of parameters has been reduced by one half from approximately 46 to 23 so that the reduction in parameter number is about 23. If desired, the comparison with a Chi-squared variate may also be used here. Unless a strong reason exists to suspect that the samples come from different populations, they may be combined. The two samples may be compared with the various results illustrated in Tables 1.1 and 1.2, with the accompanying discussion. Little reason appears to exist for suspecting that these two samples are not just different possible sets of outcomes from the same population. This result may be more apparent to the reader if the data of the second sample and of the two samples combined are grouped into intervals of $\Delta y = 20$ and the corresponding observed frequency distributions compared with that of Fig. 2.10.

An alternative procedure for this comparison is available if the second sample is also shown to have plausibly arisen from a normal (or log normal or gamma, etc.) distribution (which is the case). Then, only the two parameters, θ_1 and θ_2, need be compared using the normal (etc.) distribution likelihood function or alternatively, (normal only) first θ_2 using an F ratio, then θ_1 using a t-test. Of course, these procedures introduce additional assumptions with corresponding increase in sensitivity, but to a more limited type of difference.

Consider now the second problem mentioned at the beginning of this section. Suppose that the sociologist is studying the relationship between alcoholism and family size, that he chooses a random sample of 242 alcoholics, and determines the number of brothers and sisters of each. Kalbfleisch (1971, Chap. 8) analyzes the results provided by Sprott (1964), as given in Table 2.6. Using these data, the sociologist wishes to determine if this sample of alcoholics differs with respect to family size from the entire population (not just the population of alcoholics) of individuals in which the alcoholics live. As Kalbfleisch points out, problems arise as to what constitutes a family: the total number of children ever

TABLE 2.6

Estimated $(n.p_k)$ and observed (n_k) frequency distributions of family sizes for alcoholics. Sprott (1964) and Kalbfleisch (1971, Chap.8).

Number of siblings	0	1	2	3	4	5	6	7	8	9	10	11	12
n_k	21	32	40	47	29	23	20	11	10	3	3	3	0
$n.p_k$	34.21	51.41	47.32	37.07	26.41	17.91	12.12	7.40	4.24	2.23	1.04	0.64	

born to a mother, the number of children present in the home during the alcoholic's childhood, etc. With the assumption that the sociologist has resolved this problem in obtaining the data of Table 2.6, the hypothesis may be made that the 242 alcoholics constitute a random sample from the entire population with respect to family size. From census data, the sociologist obtains the numbers of families with each number of children in the entire population, as given in Table 2.7. Again, as Kalbfleisch points out, problems arise as to how to obtain reliable estimates of the numbers of families of each size using the definition of size decided upon for the alcoholics. With the assumption that this problem has been resolved and that Table 2.7 is representative of the entire population, the probability of an individual having k siblings must be determined. The total number of children in Table 2.7 is

$$1 \times 207{,}756 + 2 \times 156{,}111 + \dots + 12 \times 326 = 1{,}469{,}626$$

The number of children with, say, 4 siblings is $5 \times 32{,}080$, etc. The estimate of the probability that a randomly chosen member of the entire population has 4 siblings is

$$p_4 = \frac{5 \times 32{,}080}{1{,}469{,}626} = 0.11$$

TABLE 2.7

Frequency distribution of sizes of families in the overall population as derived from census data. Sprott (1964) and Kalbfleisch (1971, Chap.8).

No. of children	1	2	3	4	5
No. of families	207,756	156,111	95,779	56,275	32,080

No. of children	6	7	8	9	10	11	12
No. of families	18,128	10,511	5621	2859	1353	575	326

These may be calculated for sibling numbers from 0 to 11. Note that these are not the maximum likelihood estimates, $\hat{p}_k$, of the proportions of alcoholics with k siblings in the overall population of alcoholics. The expected number of alcoholics with each number of siblings under the hypothesis is calculated by multiplying each p_k by $n_. = 242$, as given in Table 2.6. The observed sample of alcoholics contains considerably more individuals with large families than would be expected under the hypothesis.

An alternative hypothesis is that the sample of alcoholics comes from a distinct subpopulation of alcoholics with a different probability distribution of family sizes. The maximum likelihood estimates, $\hat{p}_k$, may be calculated for the sample of alcoholics alone. For example, $\hat{p}_4 = 29/242 = 0.12$. The multinomial relative likelihood function (1.11) is used to compare the relative plausibility of the two hypotheses

$$R_M(p_k\text{'s from census data}) = 6.9 \times 10^{-9}$$

The hypothesis that family size of alcoholics is the same as in the entire population appears to be implausible. In this example, the determination of the change in the number of parameters is conceptually more difficult than before. For the second hypothesis, of a subpopulation of alcoholics, $K-1 = 11$ or more parameters must be estimated (another sample might contain alcoholics with 12 or more siblings). But, for the first hypothesis, no parameters are estimated from the data on alcoholics, all of the information coming from the census data. Thus, the difference in parameter numbers is approximately 11. The approximate Chi-squared is $-2 \log R_M = 37.6 \doteq \chi^2_{11}$ for which $p \ll 0.01$. As a result of this analysis, the sociologist may conclude that some relationship between alcoholism and family size is plausible.

This example illustrates one way in which an hypothesis about the probability distribution of labels in a population may be derived. Naturally, many others are possible and many other problems in the analysis of data from an homogeneous population may be encountered. The general procedures of this chapter should allow the sociologist to derive an analysis for a particular set of data with a wide variety of special problems.

CHAPTER 3

Dependence Analysis for Dichotomous Response Variables

3.1 Relationships among Groups

The analysis outlined in Chapter 2 may not appear to be of central importance to the sociologist since he is usually faced with much more complex situations. But these analyses do provide a firm basis from which to attack more complicated problems. For most data available to the sociologist, the distribution of responses will vary according to the circumstances in which they are produced. If these circumstances can be distinguished, the responses of all individuals under one given set of circumstances should follow some probability distribution as analyzed in the previous chapter. But, interest now lies in attempting to determine how this probability distribution changes as the circumstances change. Thus, the realm of the mathematical model is entered, as briefly discussed in Section 1.4.

From the analyses of Section 2.4, if some relationship among the probability parameters of the multinomial distribution has been found plausible, and it is thought or has been determined to hold under different conditions or circumstances, with only the parameters of the probability model varying, a mathematical model will be sought among these parameters. This case will not be discussed in what follows. Attention will be restricted to data for which only the multinomial distribution is assumed for observations under each set of circumstances. A mathematical model is sought which explains satisfactorily the differences or changes in the multinomial distribution under the various observed circumstances. And no ordering or metric need be assumed either in the responses or in the circumstances.

Suppose that the various possible responses under one of the observed sets of circumstances are y_1, y_2.... The response will vary from individual to individual so that Y is called a response or dependent variable taking the values y_1, y_2,... with probabilities p_1, p_2,... under the given set of conditions. The various conditions may also be labelled. Each type of circumstance, l, which varies may be given a set of labels: x_{l1}, x_{l2},.... Then, Y will have as many subscripts as types of circumstances. For example, in the suicide problem of the previous chapters, suppose that the conditions size of town and degree of industrialization vary. Then Y_{ij} will be the response variable describing the number of suicides in a town of size x_{1i} and degree of industrialization x_{2j}. And X_l is an independent variable taking values x_{l1}, x_{l2},... according to which circumstances of type l are encountered.

Throughout this chapter, attention will be restricted to the simple case of one dichotomous response using the binomial distribution. These analyses will be generalized to polychotomous and multivariate responses in Chapter 4.

The analysis of data which vary with the circumstances in which they are produced may be approached in two distinct ways. These will be discussed successively in the next two sections and will be seen to yield identical results. In the following sections, more complex data will be analyzed.

In the analysis of a relationship between a response or dependent variable and one or a number of independent variables, great care must be taken in making statements or inferences about dependence. The term "causal" is often used incorrectly in describing the sociological relationship, found in a given set of data, between a response distribution and the independent variables. Even although causality may exist in the *population*, the type of statement which may be made from the *data* depends on the method by which the data were collected, or on the assumptions which the sociologist is prepared to make, and not on the method of analysis.

Without *a priori* hypotheses (see Simon, 1954), a statement that an independent variable causes the response may only be made if the scientist (sociologist) has control of which individual has each value of the independent variables. He then assigns at random these values to the sample of individuals and observes the response produced. Thus, if students can be assigned at random to two different classes or schools using different teaching methods, one may infer, after a given period of time, whether or not the two methods cause different learning responses. The theory of design of experiments seeks to determine the best way in a given situation to distribute the individuals at random so that maximum information is obtained at minimum cost.

If the individuals already have fixed values of the independent variables and the scientist only selects at random which of the individuals with a given value are to be sampled, no statement of cause may be made. One can only say that an observed response distribution is associated with or dependent on the given value of the independent variables, *i.e.* describe the structure of the phenomenon in probabilistic terms. Thus, if the students are already in the two classes or schools with different teaching methods and the sociologist takes a random sample from each, he may only state whether differences in learning response are associated with or dependent on the method, but not caused by the method. The differences in ability to learn may have caused different teaching methods to be adopted or some external factor such as income level of the community may cause both differences in learning and differences in teaching. The data do not provide information about which causes which. (See the excellent discussion by Fisher (1959b) of inference-making in non-experimental research.)

Although the statements made from the data will differ depending on the method of collection, the procedures for analysis in the two cases remain identical and depend only on the structure of the data after they have been collected. All of the statistical procedures of this chapter and the next are applicable both to causal and to dependence situations. But all of the data described, except for the hospital experiment with babies (Table 3.8) of Section 3.4, yield only statements of association or dependence.

3.2 Differences among Groups

In the simplest situation, a response is measured with only two possible outcomes and under only two different circumstances. The response variable Y_i may take the two values y_{i1} and y_{i2} for each of the two conditions, $i = 1,2$. And the independent variable X_1 takes the two values x_{11} and x_{12} corresponding to the two situations. The sociologist wishes to determine if and how the probability distribution of Y_1 differs from that of Y_2, where y_{ik} has unknown probability p_{ik}.

Suppose that a random sample of individuals is chosen and that their social status is determined to be one of two possible, y_1 or y_2. Then, the probability distribution is binomial (1.3) and inferences may be made about plausible values of the proportion p_k of individuals in each category in the overall population, as in Section 1.3. But, the sociologist also has available information on the corresponding social category of the fathers of the individuals. Thus, each individual may also be classified according to his father's social category, x_{11} or x_{12}. The sociologist wishes to determine how great a difference exists between the proportion p_{1k} of individuals in category y_{1k} with fathers of category x_{11} and the proportion p_{2k} in category y_{2k} with fathers of category x_{12}.

For individuals with fathers belonging to category x_{11}, the probability distribution will be

$$Pr(n_{11}, n_{12}; p_{11}, p_{12} = 1 - p_{11}) = \binom{n_{1.}}{n_{11}} p_{11}^{n_{11}} (1 - p_{11})^{n_{12}}$$

and to category x_{12}

$$Pr(n_{21}, n_{22}; p_{21}, p_{22} = 1 - p_{21}) = \binom{n_{2.}}{n_{21}} p_{21}^{n_{21}} (1 - p_{21})^{n_{22}}$$

The question is to determine the amount of difference existing between p_{11} and p_{21}. Since the two subsamples are independent, from eqn. (1.17) the relative likelihood function for the sample is

$$R_B(p_{11}, p_{21}) = \left[\frac{p_{11}}{\hat{p}_{11}}\right]^{n_{11}} \left[\frac{1 - p_{11}}{1 - \hat{p}_{11}}\right]^{n_{12}} \left[\frac{p_{21}}{\hat{p}_{21}}\right]^{n_{21}} \left[\frac{1 - p_{21}}{1 - \hat{p}_{21}}\right]^{n_{22}} \qquad (3.1)$$

with maximum likelihood estimates $\hat{p}_{11} = n_{11}/n_{1.}$, $\hat{p}_{21} = n_{21}/n_{2.}$. From eqn. (1.18), the most useful measure of difference between the two subpopulations of individuals, those with fathers of classes x_{11} and x_{12}, is

$$\log\left[\frac{p_{11}}{1 - p_{11}}\right] - \log\left[\frac{p_{21}}{1 - p_{21}}\right] = 2\alpha_1 \qquad (3.2)$$

This parameter α_1 measures the average difference of the log of the odds or the logistic difference in the proportions between the two subpopulations. The parameter may vary between plus and minus

60

TABLE 3.1

Contingency table giving observed counts and marginal totals for one dichotomous response variable (Y) and one dichotomous independent variable (X).

X_1 \\ Y	1	2	
1	n_{11}	n_{12}	$n_{1.}$
2	n_{21}	n_{22}	$n_{2.}$
	$n_{.1}$	$n_{.2}$	$n_{..}$

infinity. The maximum likelihood estimate of α_1 is

$$\hat{\alpha}_1 = \frac{1}{2} \log\left[\frac{\hat{p}_{11}(1-\hat{p}_{21})}{\hat{p}_{21}(1-\hat{p}_{11})}\right] = \frac{1}{2}\log\left[\frac{n_{11}n_{22}}{n_{21}n_{12}}\right] \qquad (3.3)$$

The observed counts of individuals for these data may be arranged (in a contingency table) as in Table 3.1. Suppose that $\hat{\alpha}_1 = 0$ is the estimate obtained from a set of data. From eqn. (3.2) or (3.3), this implies that

$$\hat{p}_{11}(1-\hat{p}_{21}) = \hat{p}_{21}(1-\hat{p}_{11})$$

$$n_{11}n_{22} = n_{21}n_{12}$$

$$n_{11}n_{22} + (n_{11}^2 + n_{11}n_{12} + n_{11}n_{21}) = n_{21}n_{12} + (n_{11}^2 + n_{11}n_{12} + n_{11}n_{21})$$

$$n_{11}(n_{11} + n_{12} + n_{21} + n_{22}) = (n_{11} + n_{12})(n_{11} + n_{21})$$

$$n_{11} = n_{1.}n_{.1}/n_{..} \qquad (3.4)$$

Now $\hat{\alpha}_1 = 0$ also implies that $\hat{p}_{11} = \hat{p}_{21}$ or that the two sub-populations are estimated to have the same proportions of individuals in each category. In other words, the proportions of individuals observed in the two categories are independent of the category to which their father belongs. If $\hat{\alpha}_1 = 0$ or if $n_{11} = n_{1.}n_{.1}/n_{..}$, the observed values of y_{ik} are *estimated* to be independent of the values of x_{1i}. This does not imply that the variables Y and X_1 of the overall population are independent but only that the model with independence makes the observed data most probable. With $\hat{\alpha}_1 = 0$, it may also be plausible that $\alpha_1 \neq 0$ and conversely, with $\hat{\alpha}_1 \neq 0$, $\alpha_1 = 0$ may be plausible.

As given in Table 3.2, suppose that of six individuals with fathers in category 1, four sons are also in category 1; and of nine

TABLE 3.2

The observed frequency distribution of 15 sons in two social categories (Y) divided according to the two social categories (X) of their fathers.

X_1 \ Y	1	2	
1	4	2	6
2	4	5	9

individuals with fathers in category 2, five sons are also in category 2. From eqn. (3.3), the maximum likelihood estimate is $\hat{\alpha}_1 = 0.46$. Since this value is positive, it indicates that a higher proportion of individuals in category 1 than in category 2 have fathers in category 1.

The use of the formulation given in eqns. (3.2) and (3.3) (and, in general, eqn. (1.18) with the extension for polychotomous data of Chapter 4) has important practical consequences in the analysis of sociological survey data. Logically, for the determination of how the distribution of the response Y changes with the independent variable X, a number of individuals are sampled for each value of X and their response distribution, $n_{i1}/n_{i.}$, $n_{i2}/n_{i.}$, determined. Thus, the numbers of x_1 and of x_2 individuals ($n_{1.}$ and $n_{2.}$) are fixed. But, very often, an inverse sampling scheme is used so that fixed numbers of individuals are sampled for the values of the response and the value of the independent variable determined for each individual. For example, individuals are chosen according to their social category and then the social category of their fathers determined. In this case, only the proportions $n_{1k}/n_{.k}$ and $n_{2k}/n_{.k}$ can be calculated and hence estimates of the response distribution are not available. Then, for example, $\hat{p}_{11}-\hat{p}_{21}$ cannot be estimated ($n_{11}/n_{1.}-n_{21}/n_{2.}$ is meaningless). But, the logistic difference of eqns. (3.2) and (3.3) (and, by extension, all such models used in this book) can still be estimated since it involves only the ratio $n_{11}n_{22}/n_{12}n_{21}$ and not $n_{ik}/n_{i.}$. And *this difference on a logistic scale is the only one which can be estimated with inverse sampling* (see Cox, 1970, p.22). In particular, this result has important logical consequences for the construction of social mobility indices as outlined in Section 6.2.

A reformulation of the mathematical model (3.2) is useful for determining the relative likelihood function of α_1 and hence plausible values of that parameter. In order to represent the two parameters, p_{11} and p_{21}, completely (produce a saturated mathematical model), an additional parameter, say μ, may be added. Equation (3.2) may be rewritten as

$$\log \left[\frac{p_{11}}{1-p_{11}} \right] = \mu + \alpha_1$$

$$\log \left[\frac{p_{21}}{1-p_{21}} \right] = \mu - \alpha_1 \qquad (3.5)$$

These equations may be solved for p_{11} and p_{21}

$$p_{11} = \frac{e^{\mu+\alpha_1}}{1 + e^{\mu+\alpha_1}}$$

$$p_{21} = \frac{e^{\mu-\alpha_1}}{1 + e^{\mu-\alpha_1}}$$

and substituted into the relative likelihood function (3.1)

$$R_B(\mu,\alpha_1) = \frac{e^{(\mu+\alpha_1)n_{11}}}{\hat{p}_{11}{}^{n_{11}}(1-\hat{p}_{11})^{n_{12}}(1 + e^{\mu+\alpha_1})^{n_1.}}$$

$$\times \frac{e^{(\mu-\alpha_1)n_{21}}}{\hat{p}_{21}{}^{n_{21}}(1-\hat{p}_{21})^{n_{22}}(1 + e^{\mu-\alpha_1})^{n_2.}} \qquad (3.6)$$

yielding the corresponding function for these parameters. As with the one parameter relative likelihood functions considered in previous chapters, $R_B(\mu,\alpha_1)$ may take values between zero and one, larger values indicating that the corresponding pairs of parameter values are more plausible or make the data more probable. The function may be plotted as a contour map of constant values of $R_B(\mu,\alpha_1)$ on a grid of μ and α_1, as in Fig. 3.1 for the data of Table 3.2.

Inspection of this contour plot shows that the range of plausible values of α_1 varies depending on the value of μ considered. For $\mu = 1.0$, values of α_1 with relative likelihood at least 0.1 range between about -0.4 and 1.8 whereas for $\mu = -0.5$, the equivalent interval for α_1 is $(-0.7, 1.4)$. And a very large range of values of μ exists for which $\alpha_1 = 0$ is plausible. Although the most likely estimate of the effect of the father's social category is non-zero, being

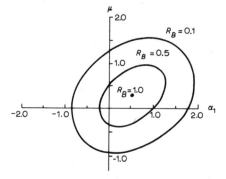

Fig. 3.1 Two contours of constant relative likelihood (0.1 and 0.5) for the two parameters of mathematical model (3.5) used to determine the plausibility of independence of the son's social category from his father's for the data of Table 3.2. All combinations of parameter values within the contour $R_B = 0.1$ make the observed data at least one tenth as probable as the maximum likelihood estimates.

$\hat{\alpha}_1 = 0.46$, the data provide no evidence that the son's social category is not independent of the father's.

Since one is primarily interested in the values of α_1 for this model, the information in Fig. 3.1 may be summarized by maxi-

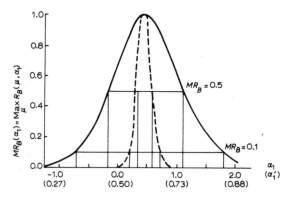

Fig. 3.2 The maximum relative likelihood graph for the difference parameter (α_1) of mathematical model (3.5) used to determine the plausibility of independence of the son's social category from his father's for the data of Tables 3.2 ($n_{..} = 15$, solid curve) and 3.3 ($n_{..} = 150$, broken curve) showing the increased precision of the inferences with increased sample size. Comparison may be made with the relative likelihood contours of Fig. 3.1. The numbers in parentheses on the horizontal axis are the values of the parameter when transformed by eqn. (3.8).

64

mizing the relative likelihood function (3.6) over μ for each fixed value of α_1, yielding the graph of Fig. 3.2. This graph is a two-dimensional profile of the three-dimensional graph of Fig. 3.1 and gives the maximum possible interval for α_1 for each relative likelihood level, no matter what value μ has, given the data. It is called the maximum relative likelihood function, MR_B, of α_1, and may be very useful especially when the model contains three or more parameters, the maximum being taken over all but one. But, the summarizing nature of this procedure should be kept in mind, since it gives only a maximum interval width for a given plausibility level; see Section 4.5 and Kalbfleisch and Sprott (1970). As before, a model with the son's class independent of the father's is very plausible in the light of the data: $MR_B(\alpha_1=0) = 0.70$.

Suppose now that 150 individuals had been sampled instead of 15 and that the results are given in Table 3.3. From eqn. (3.3), the maximum likelihood estimate $\hat{\alpha}_1 = 0.46$ is the same as previously obtained. But, as shown by the graph with the broken line in Fig. 3.2, this estimate is known with much more precision than with the previous information. Indeed, the model postulating independence is now relatively implausible: $MR_B(\alpha_1=0) = 0.02$.

The precision of the estimate should not be confused with the accuracy. The first term involves the range of values of the parameter found plausible in the light of the data and the model chosen. The accuracy depends on whether the data actually provide information about the question being asked (*e.g.* misclassification of individuals in the table leads to an inaccurate result) and on whether the model is well-chosen.

This simplest form of problem has been presented in detail because it poses virtually all of the problems to be encountered in the analysis of the relationship between one dichotomous dependent or response variable and any number of polychotomous independent variables (but not when a subrelationship of dependence

TABLE 3.3

The observed frequency distribution of 150 sons in two social categories (Y) divided according to the two social categories (X) of their fathers and giving the same estimate of independence as Table 3.2.

X_1 \ Y	1	2	
1	40	20	60
2	40	50	90

among the independent variables exists). In order to generalize, an additional redundant parameter may be introduced into eqn. (3.5)

$$\log\left[\frac{p_{i1}}{1-p_{i1}}\right] = \mu + \alpha_i \qquad (3.7)$$

where $\Sigma\alpha_i = 0$, so that $\alpha_1 = -\alpha_2$.

As noted above, the range of this parameter is $-\infty \leqslant \alpha_1 \leqslant \infty$. Since this interval is well-defined, values of α_1 from different sets of data may be compared as to size (remembering that the precision may differ). But often, a parameter varying between, say, zero and one is conceptually more convenient. Then, α_1 may be transformed into the parameter

$$\alpha_1' = \frac{e^{\alpha_1}}{1+e^{\alpha_1}} \qquad (3.8)$$

When $\alpha_1 = 0$, $\alpha_1' = 0.5$ and $0.0 \leqslant \alpha_1' \leqslant 1.0$. Since this constitutes a one-to-one relabelling of the parameter space, all of the previous results hold. For example, the new scale of the maximum relative likelihood graph is given in parentheses in Fig. 3.2. Since this scale is not linear in α_1', the graph may easily be replotted using a linear scale. If a similar transformation is applied to μ, eqn. (3.7) becomes

$$\log\left[\frac{p_{i1}}{1-p_{i1}}\right] = \log\left[\frac{\mu'}{1-\mu'}\right] + \log\left[\frac{\alpha_i'}{1-\alpha_i'}\right] \qquad (3.9)$$

where

$$\prod_i \frac{\alpha_i'}{1-\alpha_i'} = 1$$

The original formulation has several advantages in an initial analysis. In more complicated models where the parameters cannot be solved for directly but must be obtained by some numerical method of maximizing the likelihood function, as described in Appendix 2, estimation will be easier using α_1 because this parameter is not constrained to lie in a limited region (0,1). In addition, the relative likelihood graph of the parameters will usually be more symmetric using μ and α_1 than using μ' and α_1'. This is important if either approximate (Section 3.7) or more powerful (asymptotic) statistical analysis is to be applied later. In most other respects, they are identical: for example, both use all of the information in

66

the data about the difference under consideration (which is not true, in general, for the correlation and regression coefficients or other related parameters when applied to dichotomous data).

Before proceeding to more complex models, another logical approach to the problems of this chapter will be discussed in the next section.

3.3 Conditional Probability Distributions

In the previous section, the dependent variable was assumed to have a different probability distribution depending on the value of the independent variable observed. But, the independent variable may also be considered to have a probability distribution of its own. Then, why is this distribution not taken into account in the preceding analysis?

Consider the dichotomous case of fathers' (X) and sons' (Y) social categories. In the same way that the counts of sons in the two categories have a binomial distribution, so do the counts of fathers. In fact, these two distributions may be considered jointly: the probability that both father and son belong to category 1 (the proportion of families in the population with father and son in the same social category 1) is, say, q_{11}; the probability of father of category 1, son of category 2, q_{12}; etc. as illustrated in Table 3.4. The variables X and Y may be said to have a bivariate binomial distribution. The probability of observing Table 3.1 is

$$P(X, Y) = Pr(n_{11}, n_{12}, n_{21}, n_{22}; q_{11}, q_{12}, q_{21}, q_{22})$$

$$= \binom{n_{..}}{n_{11} n_{12} n_{21} n_{22}} q_{11}^{n_{11}} \, q_{12}^{n_{12}} \, q_{21}^{n_{21}} q_{22}^{n_{22}} \qquad (3.10)$$

TABLE 3.4

The parameters of the bivariate binomial distribution and of the two marginal binomial distributions.

X \ Y	1	2	
1	q_{11}	q_{12}	$q_{1.}$
2	q_{21}	q_{22}	$q_{2.}$
	$q_{.1}$	$q_{.2}$	1

with $\Sigma \Sigma q_{kl} = 1$. From Table 3.4, the marginal binomial distribution of X is

$$P(X) = Pr(n_{1.}, n_{2.}; q_{1.}, q_{2.}) = \binom{n_{..}}{n_{1.}} q_{1.}^{n_{1.}} \cdot q_{2.}^{n_{2.}} \qquad (3.11)$$

and similarly for Y. To simplify notation, $P(X, Y)$, $P(Y)$, and $P(X)$ are used respectively for the joint and the two marginal distributions of the two variables.

The parameters of Table 3.4 give the proportions of times that the possible values of the two variables occur together in the population, and thus provide the same level of analysis as the correlation coefficient when two normally distributed variables are considered. But, the sociologist is primarily interested in how the sons are distributed according to social class given the social class of their father. This may be expressed in the terminology of probability theory. Given that the variable $X = x_i$, some observed value, how is Y distributed? By definition, the conditional distribution is

$$P(Y/X) = P(X, Y)/P(X) \qquad (3.12)$$

which may be calculated using eqns. (3.10) and (3.11)

$$P(Y/X) = \binom{n_{..}}{n_{11} n_{12} n_{21} n_{22}} q_{11}^{n_{11}} q_{12}^{n_{12}} q_{21}^{n_{21}} q_{22}^{n_{22}} \bigg/ \binom{n_{..}}{n_{1.}} q_{1.}^{n_{1.}} \cdot q_{2.}^{n_{2.}}$$

$$= \binom{n_{1.}}{n_{11}} \left[\frac{q_{11}}{q_{1.}}\right]^{n_{11}} \left[\frac{q_{12}}{q_{1.}}\right]^{n_{12}} \binom{n_{2.}}{n_{21}} \left[\frac{q_{21}}{q_{2.}}\right]^{n_{21}} \left[\frac{q_{22}}{q_{2.}}\right]^{n_{22}} \qquad (3.13)$$

By comparison with the probability distribution

$$Pr(n_{11}, n_{12}, n_{21}, n_{22}; p_{11}, p_{12}=1-p_{11}, p_{21}, p_{22}=1-p_{21})$$

$$= \binom{n_{1.}}{n_{11}} p_{11}^{n_{11}} (1-p_{11})^{n_{12}} \binom{n_{2.}}{n_{21}} p_{21}^{n_{21}} (1-p_{21})^{n_{22}}$$

from which the relative likelihood function (3.1) is derived, the two distributions are identical with $p_{11} = q_{11}/q_{1.}$, and $p_{21} = q_{21}/q_{2.}$. Thus, the analysis of the previous section follows from either approach.

The probabilities p_{11} and p_{21} are called the conditional probabilities of the observed y_1 given that x_1 and x_2 respectively have been observed. Then, $P(Y/X)$ is the conditional binomial distribution of Y given X. From the development used in Section 3.2, it may be seen that the conditional distribution does not depend on any assumptions about the distribution of the independent variable(s), $P(X)$, but only on which values of the variable X have been observed. Thus, the mathematical model (3.7) may be directly extended to the cases where X is polychotomous or continuous simply by extending the index i to values greater than 2.

Conversely, the derivation of mathematical models given in Section 1.4 which resulted in models (1.18) and (1.20) rests on a firm probabilistic basis. This analysis will be useful in more complex cases, especially when a "causal" chain is considered in Section 3.5, $i.e.$ when a dependent variable at one level acts as an independent variable at another level.

3.4 Complex Models with a Dichotomous Response Variable

With one dichotomous response, the situation previously discussed may become more complex in two ways: more than one independent variable may be involved or an independent variable may take more than two values. Consider first the case of more than one independent dichotomous variable. For two independent variables, X_1 and X_2, the response variable Y_{ij} may take the values y_{ij1} and y_{ij2} for each of the four possible combinations of observed values of X_1 and X_2. Four distinct binomial distributions are to be compared under the four combinations of circumstances. With independence of observations, the probability distribution is

$$P(Y/X_1, X_2) = \prod_i \prod_j \binom{n_{ij.}}{n_{ij1}} p_{ij1}{}^{n_{ij1}} (1-p_{ij1})^{n_{ij2}} \qquad (3.14)$$

As in the simpler situation, interest lies in how the distribution of Y changes as X_1 changes and as X_2 changes. But an additional complication now enters. The distribution of Y may be affected differently by X_1 depending on the value of X_2 occurring, or conversely, $i.e.$ there may be an interaction between the two independent variables. By analogy with analysis of variance, a useful mathematical model for the analysis is

$$\log \left[\frac{p_{ij1}}{1-p_{ij1}} \right] = \mu + \alpha_i + \beta_j + \gamma_{ij} \qquad (3.15)$$

69

where

$$\sum_i \alpha_i = \sum_j \beta_j = \sum_i \gamma_{ij} = \sum_j \gamma_{ij} = 0$$

With these constraints, $\alpha_2 = -\alpha_1$, $\beta_2 = -\beta_1$, $\gamma_{12} = \gamma_{21} = -\gamma_{22} = -\gamma_{11}$ so that the model contains four parameters. The parameter α_1 gives the difference in effect between the two values of X_1, β_1 of X_2 and γ_{11} of the interaction between X_1 and X_2. If required, the transformation (3.8) may be applied to these parameters after they have been estimated.

Lazarsfeld (1955) measures the proportion of individuals who listen to religious, discussion, and classical music programmes on the radio. He considers these individuals in relation to two independent variables, their age, X_1 (young or old), and their level of education, X_2 (high or low). The data for listeners to classical music are reproduced in Table 3.5. The number of individuals observed to listen to classical music (y_{ij1}) who were old (x_{11}) with high education (x_{21}) is $n_{111} = 210$, etc. Since mathematical model (3.15) is saturated, i.e. contains as many parameters (4) as the probability distribution (3.14), the maximum likelihood estimates, $\hat{\mu}$, $\hat{\alpha}_1$, $\hat{\beta}_1$, $\hat{\gamma}_{11}$, may be obtained directly from $\hat{p}_{ij1} = n_{ij1}/n_{ij}$. by solving linear equations. Thus,

$$\log\left[\frac{\hat{p}_{111}}{1-\hat{p}_{111}}\right] = \log\left[\frac{210}{190}\right] = \hat{\mu} + \hat{\alpha}_1 + \hat{\beta}_1 + \hat{\gamma}_{11}$$

$$\log\left[\frac{\hat{p}_{121}}{1-\hat{p}_{121}}\right] = \log\left[\frac{170}{730}\right] = \hat{\mu} + \hat{\alpha}_1 - \hat{\beta}_1 - \hat{\gamma}_{11}$$

$$\log\left[\frac{\hat{p}_{211}}{1-\hat{p}_{211}}\right] = \log\left[\frac{194}{406}\right] = \hat{\mu} - \hat{\alpha}_1 + \hat{\beta}_1 - \hat{\gamma}_{11}$$

$$\log\left[\frac{\hat{p}_{221}}{1-\hat{p}_{221}}\right] = \log\left[\frac{110}{290}\right] = \hat{\mu} - \hat{\alpha}_1 - \hat{\beta}_1 + \hat{\gamma}_{11}$$

The solution of these equations is $\hat{\mu} = -0.766$, $\hat{\alpha}_1 = +0.088$, $\hat{\beta}_1 = +0.447$, and $\hat{\gamma}_{11} = +0.332$. The largest effect is due to the level of education as measured by β_1. Since this parameter is estimated to be positive, high education implies more listeners to classical music. The next effect is the interaction γ_{11} which is also estimated to be positive, implying that high education has more effect on old people listening to classical music than on young.

TABLE 3.5

The observed frequency distribution of listeners to classical music (y_{ijk}) divided according to age (x_{1i}) and educational level (x_{2j}). Lazarsfeld (1955).

	x_{21}		x_{22}	
	y_{i11}	y_{i12}	y_{i21}	y_{i22}
x_{11}	210	190	170	730
x_{12}	194	406	110	290

Finally, the effect of age, α_1, is estimated to be slightly positive, showing that higher age may imply more listeners. The same results are inferred using the transformed (eqn. (3.8)) parameters, $\hat{\alpha}'_1 = 0.522$, $\hat{\beta}'_1 = 0.608$, and $\hat{\gamma}'_{11} = 0.582$, remembering that these may vary between zero and one, with the turning point at 0.5.

The question now arises as to whether the data actually support these effects or if the parameters measuring the differences might plausibly be considered to be zero. The relative likelihood function is obtained from the probability distribution (3.14) after substitution of the mathematical model (3.15)

$$R_B(\mu,\alpha_1,\beta_1,\gamma_{11}) =$$

$$\prod_i \prod_j \frac{\exp[(\mu+\alpha_i+\beta_j+\gamma_{ij})n_{ij1}]}{\hat{p}_{ij1}^{n_{ij1}}(1-\hat{p}_{ij1})^{n_{ij2}}[1 + \exp(\mu+\alpha_i+\beta_j+\gamma_{ij})]^{n_{ij}}} \quad (3.16)$$

with the constraints of eqn. (3.15). For this model, the usefulness of the maximum relative likelihood function, maximized over all parameters but one, becomes evident.

When this function is plotted for each of the three parameters of interest, the graphs are all found to be narrow, providing a small range of plausible values of the parameters. The plausibilities of the parameters β_1 and γ_{11}, but not that of α_1, being zero, as measured by MR_B, are very close to zero, i.e. the data provide no evidence that the proportion of listeners to classical music varies with age but only with educational level, this level having more effect on older individuals. Approximate analyses of these data are given in Sections 3.7 and 4.2. (See Tables 3.12 and 4.5.)

As in the simpler model of Section 3.2, the measure of plausibility that a parameter is zero may be more important than the actual maximum likelihood estimate of the parameter. One pa-

71

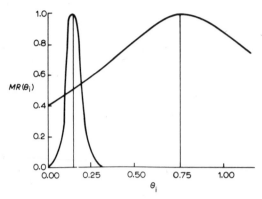

Fig. 3.3 The maximum relative likelihood graphs for two parameters in a model which are estimated with different precisions. The parameter estimated to be far from zero could very plausibly be zero whereas the parameter estimated to be close to zero is implausibly actually zero.

rameter, estimated to be very close to zero, may have a very low plausibility of being actually zero (a very narrow likelihood graph) whereas another parameter in the same model with the same data which is estimated to be much further from zero may have a high plausibility of being zero, as illustrated in Fig. 3.3. Although the first effect is estimated as being much less than the second, the plausibility, according to the data, of the first effect actually existing is much greater than the second. These considerations are exemplified by normal theory analysis of variance (of which the preceding is the binomial distribution analogue) for which only levels of plausibility (as expressed by F values) are often given with no indication of estimated parameter values, a practice which also should be avoided. In the preceding example, the opposite result has arisen. The parameter close to zero, α_1, has a wider graph than the other two.

Consider now the second way in which the simple model of Section 3.2 may become more complex: an independent variable may take more than two values. Suppose that a question with possible responses (Y) yes and no is posed to workers with less than one year (x_{21}) and with more than five years (x_{22}) experience on the job. Two similar factories are sampled, each containing both men and women, so that a second independent variable (X_1) is constructed with x_{11} and x_{12} signifying men and women of the first factory, x_{13} and x_{14} of the second factory, respectively. This simple structure has been used, instead of introducing two

72

TABLE 3.6

The observed frequency distributions of responses to a yes/no question (y_{ijk}) divided according to factory (x_{11}, x_{12} and x_{13}, x_{14}), sex (x_{11}, x_{13} and x_{12}, x_{14}), and experience (x_{2j}). Adapted from biological data of Gart (1971).

	x_{21}		x_{22}	
	y_{i11}	y_{i12}	y_{i21}	y_{i22}
x_{11}	5	74	4	12
x_{12}	3	84	2	14
x_{13}	10	80	4	14
x_{14}	3	79	1	14

additional variables for sex and factory, because primary interest lies in the effect of experience. Although more detailed analysis would require use of three independent variables, experience, sex, and factory, this less complex analysis will be seen to provide information on differences between sexes and between factories, but not on interaction between sex and factory. The results, adapted from a biological example of Gart (1971), are given in Table 3.6. In this situation, the sociologist is primarily interested in how different are the responses with experience, after removing effects of sex and factory. If the index i is extended to four possible values, eqn. (3.15) may be used in the analysis of these data, along with the corresponding relative likelihood function (3.16).

Instead of proceeding directly to the estimation of the parameters of the model, first consider the plausibility of some simpler models. The simplest model assumes that the same distribution of responses is found no matter which combination of experience—sex—factory the individual questioned has. The corresponding mathematical model is

$$\log \left[\frac{p_{ij1}}{1 - p_{ij1}} \right] = \mu \quad \text{(all } i,j) \tag{3.17}$$

The relative plausibility of this model is given by $R_B(\tilde{\mu}$, $\alpha_i=0, \beta_1=0, \gamma_{i1}=0) = 5.3 \times 10^{-4}$ with a reduction from eight to one parameter. Note that the maximum likelihood estimate $\tilde{\mu}$ from this model differs from that, $\hat{\mu}$, in the saturated model (3.15). Even with the elimination of seven parameters, some overall effect seems to be present (the model is implausible). This effect may arise from difference in experience, difference in sex—factory, in-

73

teraction between experience and sex—factory, or from some combination of these.

Since the interaction effect is of least interest, suppose that it is eliminated from the model. The interaction is measured by three parameters, γ_{11}, γ_{21}, γ_{31}, say, with the five remaining values given by the constraints. If no interaction effect is present, all of these parameters will be zero, giving the model

$$\log\left[\frac{p_{ij1}}{1-p_{ij1}}\right] = \mu + \alpha_i + \beta_j \qquad (3.18)$$

where $\Sigma\alpha_i = \Sigma\beta_j = 0$. The plausibility of this model is given by $R_B(\tilde{\mu},\tilde{\alpha}_i,\tilde{\beta}_1,\gamma_{i1}=0) = 0.65$. (Again, $\tilde{\mu}$ and $\tilde{\alpha}_i$ denote the maximum likelihood estimates obtained from eqn. (3.18) and not those from eqn. (3.15) which will be given below.) With the elimination of three parameters, this model with no interaction is very plausible. The response may be assumed to depend on the amount of experience in the same way for both sexes and both factories.

The two effects of interest now remain to be considered. Depending on the plausibility of the previous model (3.18) analyzed, one of two different models will be used for each effect. Both will be given here for completeness, although only the second is needed for this example because of the lack of evidence of an interaction effect.

If the interaction is found to be plausible and the sociologist wishes to determine the plausibility of differences in response according to the combination of sex—factory, he hypothesizes that the differences, as measured by the three parameters, α_1, α_2, α_3 (α_4 given by the constraints) are zero in model (3.15) yielding

$$\log\left[\frac{p_{ij1}}{1-p_{ij1}}\right] = \mu + \beta_j + \gamma_{ij} \qquad (3.19)$$

where

$$\sum_j \beta_j = \sum_i \gamma_{ij} = \sum_j \gamma_{ij} = 0$$

The relative plausibility of this model compared with (3.15) is $R_B(\tilde{\mu},\alpha_1 = 0,\tilde{\beta}_1,\tilde{\gamma}_{i1}) = 0.051$ with the elimination of three parameters. This value may be considered on the border of plausibility. In the same way, for plausibility of difference in response by experience, the one parameter β_1 may be set equal to zero, giving the model

$$\log \left[\frac{p_{ij1}}{1-p_{ij1}}\right] = \mu + \alpha_i + \gamma_{ij} \qquad (3.20)$$

where

$$\sum_i \alpha_i = \sum_i \gamma_{ij} = \sum_j \gamma_{ij} = 0$$

with relative plausibility $R_B(\tilde{\mu}, \tilde{\alpha}_i, \beta_1 = 0, \; \tilde{\gamma}_{i1}) = 0.094$ compared with model (3.15), with one parameter eliminated. Since three differences are measured among sex—factory combinations but only one for experience, the plausibility of difference due to expe- rience may be considered slightly greater than that due to sex— factory combinations, although the relative likelihoods are the reverse. (As in previous chapters, $-2 \log MR$ may be compared approximately to a Chi-squared variate.)

Since the interaction effect has been found implausible in the example, model (3.15) may be replaced by model (3.18) in the determination of the effects of experience and sex—factory. In this case, the relative likelihood function (3.16) must be replaced by

$$R_{NI}(\mu, \alpha_i, \beta_1) =$$

$$\prod_i \prod_j \left[\frac{\exp(\mu+\alpha_i+\beta_j)}{\exp(\tilde{\mu}+\tilde{\alpha}_i+\tilde{\beta}_j)}\right]^{n_{ij1}} \left[\frac{1+\exp(\tilde{\mu}+\tilde{\alpha}_i+\tilde{\beta}_j)}{1+\exp(\mu+\alpha_i+\beta_j)}\right]^{n_{ij.}} \qquad (3.21)$$

where $\tilde{\mu}$, $\tilde{\alpha}_i$, $\tilde{\beta}_j$ are the maximum likelihood estimates obtained from mathematical model (3.18), i.e. with $\gamma_{ij} = 0$, and not from model (3.15). For the plausibility of difference in sex—factory and in experience respectively affecting the response, models (3.19) and (3.20) are replaced by

$$\log \left[\frac{p_{ij1}}{1-p_{ij1}}\right] = \mu + \beta_j \qquad (3.22)$$

with $\Sigma \beta_j = 0$, and

$$\log \left[\frac{p_{ij1}}{1-p_{ij1}}\right] = \mu + \alpha_i \qquad (3.23)$$

with $\Sigma \alpha_i = 0$. The resulting plausibilities are $R_{NI}(\tilde{\mu}, \alpha_i=0, \tilde{\beta}_1) = 0.027$, with elimination of three parameters, for differences in sex—factory, and $R_{NI}(\tilde{\mu}, \tilde{\alpha}_1, \beta_1 = 0) = 0.031$, with elimination of

TABLE 3.7

The likelihood analysis of the responses to a yes/no question given in Table 3.6 using log maximum relative likelihoods to determine effect of differences in sex—factory and experience.

Model	$\log MR_B$		Change in number of parameters
	No interaction (3.18)	Interaction (3.15)	
Overall	−7.14	−7.57	7
Between sex—factories	−3.62	−2.98	3
Between experiences	−3.48	−2.36	1
Interaction		−0.43	3

one parameter, for differences in experience. These likelihoods confirm the results given above that, taking into account the number of differences (parameters eliminated), an effect of experience on the response is more plausible than that of sex—factory. These results are summarized in Table 3.7 using natural logarithms of the maximum relative likelihoods.

With mathematical model (3.15), the maximum likelihood estimates may be obtained by solving linear equations, as with the data of Table 3.5. The estimates so obtained are

$$\hat{\mu} = -2.289 \qquad \hat{\alpha}_1 = +0.393 \qquad \hat{\gamma}_{11} = -\hat{\gamma}_{12} = -0.243$$
$$\hat{\beta}_1 = -\hat{\beta}_2 = -0.555 \qquad \hat{\alpha}_2 = -0.350 \qquad \hat{\gamma}_{21} = -\hat{\gamma}_{22} = -0.138$$
$$\hat{\alpha}_3 = +0.623 \qquad \hat{\gamma}_{31} = -\hat{\gamma}_{32} = +0.142$$
$$\hat{\alpha}_4 = -0.666 \qquad \hat{\gamma}_{41} = -\hat{\gamma}_{42} = +0.239$$

Inspection of these estimates provides a different type of information about the data than does the likelihood analysis of Table 3.7. Although the interaction parameters are somewhat closer to zero than the other estimates, these values provide no reason to suppose that the parameters might actually be zero. But, the likelihood analysis has shown that they may very plausibly be zero. Of the remaining parameters, the most interesting result is that the sex—factory variable is dichotomized as might be expected, with a difference in response between men and women, the difference being greater in the second factory. If the sociologist is interested in this problem, he may perform a more detailed analysis by splitting the variable X_1 into two variables, for sex and for factory respectively, and redoing the analysis. More simply, for example, the relative likelihood, (3.21) in this case, may be considered successively with $\alpha_1 = \alpha_2 = 0$ and then with $\alpha_3 = \alpha_4 = 0$ to determine which factory plausibly has the greatest effect on the response. Another model to be considered is that with $\alpha_1 = -\alpha_2$, $\alpha_3 = -\alpha_4$, which is found to have relative likelihood almost one.

The estimation of the parameters in mathematical models (3.18)—(3.20) involves the solution of non-linear equations obtained by equating to zero the first partial derivatives, with respect to each remaining parameter, of the log (relative) likelihood function obtained from eqn. (3.16) after setting the appropriate parameters to zero (see Appendix 2). In contrast, models (3.22) and (3.23) yield easily solved linear equations, since they are equivalent to model (3.7), as does model (3.15). Programmes for this estimation problem, providing the likelihood analysis of Table 3.7, are available in Lindsey (1971) when one or two independent variables are associated with a dichotomous response variable. Goodman (1972) uses the models of this section but makes the error of estimating the parameters of (3.18) from the marginal frequencies of the observed table *i.e.* from eqns. (3.22) and (3.23).

The best way to determine how sex, factory, and experience affect the response is to inspect the surface defined by the relative likelihood function. Since this surface is multidimensional, the maximum relative likelihood functions may be used. Five graphs may be plotted in this example: for α_1, α_2, α_3, α_4, (one being redundant) and for β_1 (that for β_2 being symmetric). Comparison

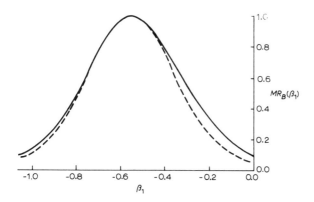

Fig. 3.4 The maximum relative likelihood graph to determine the plausibility of a difference in the distribution of responses to a question with experience when the interaction with factory—sex is allowed for (solid curve, mathematical model (3.15)) and not allowed for (broken curve, model (3.18)).

77

of these will provide most of the information required about effects measured from these data. Since difference in response with experience is central in this example, only the graph for this parameter, β_1, is provided here, in Fig. 3.4. Graphs are plotted for the two models, with (3.15) and without (3.18) interaction. The maximum likelihood estimates may be seen to be indistinguishable in the two cases, but the plausibility of the parameters being zero differs, as summarized in Table 3.7. The no-interaction model gives a slightly narrower range of plausible values of β_1.

One additional problem appears to arise when this form of logistic analysis is applied to data. If all of the individuals in one cell of a table (under one set of circumstances) provide the same response, $\log[\hat{p}/(1-\hat{p})]$ will be plus or minus infinity. Then, the parameters of model (3.15) are ill-defined and cannot be estimated. But, the estimates $\hat{p}_{ij1}$ are still defined so that the relative likelihood function may be used. Unless all of the individuals for one value of an independent variable give the same response (e.g. in Table 3.6, all experienced workers answer y_{i12} to the question so that the column y_{i11} is zero), all of the other models (3.17) to (3.23) may be used. (Note that $p^0 = 0^0 = 1$.) Thus, although the parameters of the mathematical model cannot be estimated (a reparametrization with reduction in number would allow estimation), the plausibility of the effects may be determined using the relative likelihood function, as will be illustrated by the following example.

An experiment is performed in a hospital, as discussed by Cox (1966, 1970), to determine the effect of attention paid to babies. Each day for 18 days (X_1), one baby is chosen at random from those present and not crying and rocked for a fixed period. At the end of the period, the number of babies crying in the experimental (rocked, x_{21}) and control (not rocked, x_{22}) groups are counted. The results are provided in Table 3.8. This is an extreme case of the above-mentioned phenomenon since the estimated probability of crying for the rocked babies each day must be either zero or one. This is also an example to which the term causal might be applied if the effect of rocking is found to be plausible, since the experimenter has control of which individual babies will be rocked.

Application of the same analysis as for the previous example, without detailed discussion, gives the results summarized in Table 3.9. Since the interaction between the treatment and the day and the differences among days are not of primary interest, elimi-

TABLE 3.8

The observed frequency distributions of babies crying (y_{ijk}) on 18 days in an experiment to determine the effect of rocking. Cox (1966, 1970).

Day (x_{1i})	Experimental (rocked x_{21})		Control (not rocked x_{22})	
	Not crying	Crying	Not crying	Crying
1	1	0	3	5
2	1	0	2	4
3	1	0	1	4
4	0	1	1	5
5	1	0	4	1
6	1	0	4	5
7	1	0	5	3
8	1	0	4	4
9	1	0	3	2
10	0	1	8	1
11	1	0	5	1
12	1	0	8	1
13	1	0	5	3
14	1	0	4	1
15	1	0	4	2
16	1	0	7	1
17	0	1	4	2
18	1	0	5	3

nation of these parameters is considered first. Each involves the elimination of 17 parameters so that neither effect of interaction nor of days need be considered plausible, although the relative likelihoods are fairly small. One may then proceed to the effect of rocking using the no-interaction model and see that the elimina-

TABLE 3.9

Likelihood analysis of the data on the effect of rocking on babies crying given in Table 3.8.

Model	log MR_B		Change in number of parameters
	No interaction (3.18)	Interaction (3.15)	
Overall effect	−15.08	−23.23	35
Rocking	−2.33	−0.00	1
Between days	−13.28	−5.10	17
Interaction		−8.15	17

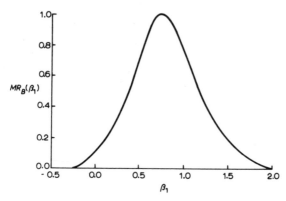

Fig. 3.5 The maximum relative likelihood graph to determine the plausibility of a difference in crying response of babies when rocked with interaction with days not allowed for.

tion of this one parameter is on the border of implausibility. The maximum relative likelihood function of this parameter, β_1, using the no-interaction model (3.18), is plotted in Fig. 3.5. With this model, the maximum likelihood estimate is $\hat{\beta}_1 = 0.70$, indicating that rocking may increase the number of babies not crying. From eqn. (3.2), the estimated relationship between the proportion of rocked (p_1) and unrocked (p_2) babies not crying is approximately $p_1 = 4p_2/(1+3p_2)$, after differences among days have been removed.

But the reader may have noticed a peculiarity of the analysis in Table 3.9. With the interaction model, an effect due to rocking seems to have absolutely no support (the parameter may be eliminated), since the relative likelihood is one. Further investigation reveals that the graph of β_1 for the interaction model (3.15) is completely flat, the relative likelihood being one for all values of β_1. This indicates that, if the interaction of the experiment with days were supported, $i.e.$ if the effect of rocking varied with the day, no information would be provided by the data about plausible values of β_1, $i.e.$ about presence and size of the effect of rocking. Since interaction is not supported by the data, information about β_1 provided by the no-interaction model and summarized in Fig. 3.4 would be confounded with the interaction and lost if the interaction model were used. The possibility of this problem arising could have been avoided by designing the experiment so that more babies were rocked each day.

This example illustrates an important reason for inspecting the likelihood surface and not simply the values of the relative likelihood when certain parameters are set equal to zero, as given in a table such as 3.7 or 3.9. The log relative likelihood equal to zero in Table 3.9 seems to imply that the parameter β_1 may plausibly be assumed to be zero (as it can, but no more plausibly than any non-zero value). But, in fact, the data provide no information about the value of β_1 in this model.

After studying the analyses of the three examples provided in this section, the reader should be in a position to perform the analysis on any similar set of data with a single dichotomous response variable and a number of polychotomous independent variables. The more independent variables are introduced and the more values each can take, the larger the sample of individuals required in order to have usable information about all of the effects to be studied. In the previous example, an insufficient number of babies rocked was sampled to allow determination of plausibility of the effect sought.

As an example of a more complex situation, the mathematical model when three independent variables (X_1, X_2, X_3) are measured may be

$$\log \left[\frac{p_{ijl1}}{1 - p_{ijl1}} \right] = \mu + \alpha_i + \beta_j + \delta_l + \gamma_{ij} + \epsilon_{il} + \phi_{jl} + \eta_{ijl} \qquad (3.24)$$

with summation for each parameter set over each index equal to zero, and where each index takes as many values as the corresponding variable. A complex example such as this will be analyzed in Section 3.7. Such complex and specialized models may be found in any book on design and analysis of experiments, such as Cochran and Cox (1966). In these books, the models used explain variation in the mean of a normal distribution under varying circumstances.

3.5 Complex Dependence Relationships

As the sociological data becomes more complex and more independent variables are added, subsystems of relationships among variables may appear. The manner in which the distributions of one or more of these independent variables change as other independent variables take different values may be of interest to the sociologist. A system of "causal" chains or a dependence network may appear to be described by the phenomena under study. In the example taken from Lazarsfeld on the listeners to classical music, the sociologist might also be interested in the dependence of educational level on age. Boudon (1971) gives a detailed discussion of dependence analysis for dichotomous data, but unfortunately uses the very approximate method of assuming the proportion of responses to be normally distributed (the approximation is reasonable for p_1 close to 0.5 in all cells of a table, but requires very large values of n in cells with p_1 near 0 or 1; see Section 3.7 and Kalbfleisch, 1971, Chap. 4). However, he does use, implicitly, a measure of plausibility of an effect being zero, since the distance from zero of his standardized "dependence" coefficients, which are in effect standardized regression coefficients from normal distribution or "least squares" theory, is proportional to the plausibility of their being zero.

As in the examples of Section 3.4, suppose that two independent variables (X_1, X_2) affect the distribution of the dependent variable (Y). The joint trivariate distribution of Y, X_1, and X_2 in these examples is

$$P(Y, X_1, X_2) = P(Y/X_1, X_2)P(X_1, X_2) \qquad (3.25)$$

where the term $P(Y/X_1, X_2)$ was used in deriving the mathematical models. Now, suppose that the distribution of X_2 depends on the value of the variable X_1 observed. The remaining term $P(X_1, X_2)$ of eqn. (3.25) contains all of the information in the data about this second dependence relationship and can be decomposed using eqn. (3.12). Equation (3.25) may be rewritten

$$P(Y, X_1, X_2) = P(Y/X_1, X_2)P(X_2/X_1)P(X_1) \qquad (3.26)$$

and the terms $P(Y/X_1, X_2)$ and $P(X_2/X_1)$ used to analyze completely the relationship among the three variables. In other words, if Y and X_2 are both dichotomous, the analysis of Section 3.4 is applied to the dependence of Y on X_1 and X_2 and that of Section 3.2 to the dependence of X_2 on X_1.

For the data of Lazarsfeld, the first part of this analysis was given in the previous section. Consider now the dependence of educational level on age. The marginal sums obtained from Table 3.5 are the relevant data, as given in Table 3.10. Obviously, these data were not obtained in order to study the relationship between age and education. The numbers provided in Table 3.10 do not represent a random sample from the population consisting of the two age groups and educational levels. But, for the sake of illustration, the counts may be assumed to represent approximate-

TABLE 3.10

Marginal totals from Table 3.5 giving the observed distribution of educational levels (x_{1i}) divided according to age (x_{2i}). Lazarsfeld (1955).

	x_{11}	x_{12}
x_{21}	400	600
x_{22}	900	400

ly the population. The application of the analysis of Section 3.2 using model (3.7) gives the maximum likelihood estimates $\hat{\mu}$ = -0.203, $\hat{\alpha}_1$ = -0.608, showing that the level of education decreases with age. The relative likelihood graph of α_1 is very narrow because of the large numbers of individuals observed and $\alpha_1 = 0$ is very implausible. (This example illustrates well the difference between accuracy and precision: the estimate of difference in education with age is determined very precisely by the data but this estimate is not at all accurate because the data were not randomly chosen from the population.)

Without confusing the α_1 of Section 3.4 representing the dependence of listening to classical music on age with the α_1 given above representing the dependence of education on age, the results of the dependence analysis may be summarized as follows.

Education level

$\hat{\alpha}_1 = -0.608$ decreases with age;

listeners to classical music

$\hat{\alpha}_1$ = +0.088   not affected by age,
$\hat{\beta}_1$ = +0.447   increase with educational level,
$\hat{\gamma}_{11}$ = +0.332   increase more with high education and older age than with high education and younger age.

Since all of these estimates are known very precisely (all relative likelihood graphs are narrow), these values summarize a large part of the information in the data about the effects under study.

In some situations, it may appear equally possible to assume that X_1 depends on X_2 or that X_2 depends on X_1, $i.e.$ to consider $P(X_1/X_2)$ or $P(X_2/X_1)$. Although the joint distribution $P(Y,X_1,X_2)$ can only be decomposed so as to contain either one or the other conditional probability, comparison of the two analyses may yield useful information. Similarly, a decomposition cannot contain both $P(Y/X_1,X_2)$ and, say, $P(X_2/Y,X_1)$ simultaneously.

83

When a conditional distribution is used in any statistical analysis of data, extreme care must be taken to observe the decomposition rules since otherwise contradictions will appear in inferences made.

As more variables are introduced into the analysis, consideration of the decomposition becomes more imperative. With four variables, the decomposition is

$$P(Y,X_1,X_2,X_3) = P(Y/X_1,X_2,X_3)P(X_3/X_1,X_2)P(X_2/X_1)P(X_1)$$

$$(3.27)$$

In this case, one, two, or three of the conditional distributions may be relevant for a given problem. For example, Y may depend on X_1, X_2, and X_3 and X_2 on X_1 with X_3 being independent of X_1 and X_2.

Two variables are defined to be independent if

$$P(X_1,X_2) = P(X_1)P(X_2) \qquad (3.28)$$

which, from eqn. (3.12), implies that

$$P(X_1/X_2) = P(X_1) \qquad P(X_2/X_1) = P(X_2) \qquad (3.29)$$

This condition holds if all of the parameters in the mathematical model related to the independent variable (including interactions) are zero. If these parameters are all plausibly zero, the hypothesis of independence between the two variables is said to be plausible. For example, the model (3.15) is represented by $P(Y/X_1,X_2)$. If β_j and γ_{ij} may plausibly be zero (for all i and j) as determined from the data, the conditional distribution of Y is plausibly independent of X_2 or the dependence of the distribution of Y on the value of X_2 is not supported by the data.

If the hypothesis that X_3 is independent of X_1 and X_2 is true, eqn. (3.27) becomes

$$P(Y,X_1,X_2,X_3) = P(Y/X_1,X_2,X_3)P(X_3)P(X_2/X_1)P(X_1) \quad (3.30)$$

If each variable is independent of all others in the chain, except one, the decomposition becomes

$$P(Y,X_1,X_2,X_3) = P(Y/X_3)P(X_3/X_2)P(X_2/X_1)P(X_1) \qquad (3.31)$$

It is always preferable to begin with the hypothesis of maximum dependence as expressed by eqn. (3.27), if all of these dependence relations make sociological sense, and then to determine the plausibility of the appropriate parameters being zero, thus seeing if a system such as (3.30) or (3.31) is plausible. Note that if a variable depends on more than one other, the corresponding conditional probability distribution in general includes all possible interactions. (The normal distribution is a notable exception to this statement because of its unique properties.)

These results hold, in general, even when the variables, including Y, are polychotomous or continuous. Thus, some means of analyzing the dependence relationship when the response is not dichotomous is required. If the response variable may be assumed to have a normal distribution, normal theory regression and analysis of variance are used. But since only count data are under consideration here, a generalization of the procedures of Section 3.4 to polychotomous response data will be developed in Chapter 4.

3.6 Regression Models

In all of the previous analyses of this chapter, no assumption has been made that the independent variables are ordered, composed of counts or measures (although, of course, they may be). If they are of this form, the sociologist may wish to devise a mathematical model describing how the distribution of the dichotomous response variable changes with different values of the independent variables, instead of only measuring differences in the response distribution. For example, some relationship may be postulated between the age of respondents and their response to a yes/no question without grouping the ages. As previously, the logistic form will often be the logical choice for such models. Two simple models are

$$\log \left[\frac{p_{i1}}{1-p_{i1}} \right] = \alpha + \beta x_{1i} \quad \text{or} \quad \frac{p_{i1}}{1-p_{i1}} = \alpha' \exp(\beta x_{1i}) \quad (3.32)$$

and

$$\log \left[\frac{p_{i1}}{1-p_{i1}} \right] = \alpha + \beta \log x_{1i} \quad \text{or} \quad \frac{p_{i1}}{1-p_{i1}} = \alpha' x_{1i}^{\beta} \quad (3.33)$$

where $\alpha' = e^{\alpha}$. As mentioned in Section 1.4, an advantage of models such as these is that, no matter what values of α and β are estimated, no value of X_1 will yield an estimate of the proportion p_{i1} outside the interval $(0,1)$. In the second model (3.33), X_1 must, of course, always be positive.

85

The extension of such models to data with more independent variables is straightforward, the models being formed in the same way as with normal theory regression analysis. For example, with two independent variables, X_1 and X_2, eqn. (3.32) might become

$$\log \left[\frac{p_{ij1}}{1 - p_{ij1}} \right] = \alpha + \beta_1 x_{1i} + \beta_2 x_{2i} + \beta_3 x_{1i} x_{2i} \qquad (3.34)$$

where the parameter β_3 measures the *linear* interaction between X_1 and X_2. Terms such as $\beta_4 x_{1i}^2$, $\beta_5 x_{1i}^3$, etc. may also be added if required, often using orthogonal polynomials (see the next section), as long as the highest power is at least one less than the number of different values of the corresponding independent variable observed.

If the independent variable X_1 is dichotomous, the model (3.32) is exactly equivalent to eqn. (3.7). If both X_1 and X_2 are dichotomous, model (3.34) is equivalent to eqn. (3.15). These relationships may be seen by letting the dichotomous variables X_1 and X_2 take the values ± 1.

With regression models, reasons often appear for not using a linear logistic model such as those described above. If $\hat{p}_{ij1} = n_{ij1} / n_{ij}$ does not approach zero or one for any values of the independent variables, and if the behaviour of this proportion is not important at these boundaries, the sociologist may be able to develop a theoretical mathematical model in the region of interest. One example of this is an explanation of voting behaviour.

Suppose that the response Y is a vote for or against (*i.e.* for another) a given party in an election. In the absence of knowledge of how lower class people voted, the sociologist may try to reconstruct the situation by using as the explanatory variable the proportion of people in the lower class in the community. Boudon (1970, Chap. V) provides a number of possible simple models to describe the relationship. In the simplest model, the proportion of the lower class voting for the party remains constant from community to community as does the corresponding proportion of the upper class. The model is then

$$p_{i1} = \alpha + \beta x_{1i} \qquad (3.35)$$

Rewritten as

$$p_{i1} = (\alpha + \beta) x_{1i} + \alpha (1 - x_{1i}) \qquad (3.36)$$

$(\alpha + \beta)$ describes the proportion of the lower class voting for the party and α of the upper class. If $\beta \leqslant 1$ is implausible, the model must be rejected since this parameter, as a difference in proportions, cannot be greater than one. (Note that $\hat{\beta}$ may still be greater than one without rejecting the model.) Plausibility statements are made by substituting the model (3.35) into the relative likelihood function (1.17).

If the second power of the independent variable is added

$$p_{i1} = \alpha_1 + \beta_1 x_{1i} + \beta_2 x_{1i}^2 \tag{3.37}$$

the model may be interpreted as showing that the proportion of each class voting for the party increases linearly with increase in the proportion of lower class members in the community

$$\alpha + \beta = a_1 + b_1 x_{1i}$$

$$\alpha = a_2 + b_2 x_{1i}$$

from eqn. (3.36), where $\alpha_1 = a_2$, $\beta_1 = a_1 - a_2 + b_2$ and $\beta_2 = b_1 - b_2$, from eqn. (3.37). Of course, the parameters a_1, b_1, and b_2 cannot be estimated separately without further hypotheses.

A third possible model

$$p_{i1} = \frac{\alpha_3 + \beta_3 x_{1i}}{\alpha_4 + \beta_4 x_{1i}} \tag{3.38}$$

may be interpreted to mean that the proportion of each class voting for the party increases linearly with the total proportion of votes for the party in the community

$$\alpha + \beta = a_1 + b_1 p_{i1}$$

$$\alpha = a_2 + b_2 p_{i1}$$

where $\alpha_3 = a_1$, $\beta_3 = a_1 - a_2$, $\alpha_4 = 1 - b_2$, and $\beta_4 = b_2 - b_1$. In this case, all of the parameters, a_1, a_2, b_1, b_2 may be determined.

Inferences about any of the parameters in these models, including a_i, b_i, are made after substituting the appropriate mathematical model (3.35), (3.37), or (3.38) into the relative likelihood function (1.17).

For a number of reasons, models such as used in this last example are specialized and do not lead to a general treatment: an interpretable model is sought which is acceptable for the specific problem. In this example, information was not available about how the lower class actually voted; the various models attempt to

87

reconstruct this missing information using a variety of hypotheses. An example of a more complex general problem, using an extension of the model (3.32), will be discussed in the second example of the next section.

3.7 Further Examples

After this development of the basic concepts of dependence analysis with a dichotomous response variable, consideration of a more complex problem is useful to determine how much information can be obtained without resorting to computer calculations.

TABLE 3.11

The observed distribution of good (n_1) and bad scores on a test for knowledge of cancer divided according to exposure to newspapers (a), radio (b), solid reading (c), and lectures (d). The estimated proportion of good scores, the log odds, and an estimate of variance are given. Lombard and Doering (1947).

	1	a	b	ab
n_1	84	75	13	35
n_2	393	156	50	59
$\hat{p}_1$	0.1761	0.3246	0.2063	0.3723
$log\,(n_1/n_2)$	−1.5430	−0.7324	−1.3471	−0.5222
Variance	0.0144	0.0196	0.0925	0.0449

	c	ac	bc	abc
n_1	67	201	16	102
n_2	83	177	16	67
$\hat{p}_1$	0.4467	0.5317	0.5000	0.6036
$log\,(n_1/n_2)$	−0.2142	0.1272	0.0000	0.4203
Variance	0.0268	0.0106	0.1211	0.0234

	d	ad	bd	abd
n_1	2	7	4	8
n_2	10	6	3	4
$\hat{p}_1$	0.1667	0.5385	0.5714	0.6667
$log\,(n_1/n_2)$	−1.6094	0.1542	0.2877	0.6932
Variance	0.4600	0.2882	0.5130	0.2399

	cd	acd	bcd	abcd
n_1	3	27	1	23
n_2	8	18	3	8
$\hat{p}_1$	0.2727	0.6000	0.2500	0.7419
$log\,(n_1/n_2)$	−0.9808	0.4055	−1.0986	1.0561
Variance	0.3030	0.0904	0.9380	0.1580

Lombard and Doering (1947) give data about knowledge of cancer as measured by a good or a bad score on a test. The individuals are classified as to presence or absence of exposure to four factors: A, newspapers; B, radio; C, solid reading and D, lectures. In Table 3.11, the individuals are labelled with the letters a, b, c, d only if exposed to the corresponding factor, e.g. ad means exposed to newspapers and lectures but not to radio and solid reading. There are four dichotomous independent variables and one dichotomous response variable. With four independent variables, interactions up to order three may be calculated using the mathematical model

$$\log\left[\frac{p_{ijlm1}}{p_{ijlm2}}\right] = \mu + \alpha_i + \beta_j + \gamma_l + \delta_m + (\alpha\beta)_{ij} + (\alpha\gamma)_{il} + (\alpha\delta)_{im}$$

$$+ (\beta\gamma)_{jl} + (\beta\delta)_{jm} + (\gamma\delta)_{lm} + (\alpha\beta\gamma)_{ijl} + (\alpha\beta\delta)_{ijm}$$

$$+ (\alpha\gamma\delta)_{ilm} + (\beta\gamma\delta)_{jlm} + (\alpha\beta\gamma\delta)_{ijlm} \qquad (3.39)$$

With the usual summation over the two values of each index of each parameter equal to zero, this model contains 16 parameters. Since the model is saturated, the maximum likelihood estimates of the parameters may be obtained, as in Section 3.4, by solving linear equations using the values of $\log(n_1/n_2)$ for each cell of Table 3.11 and yielding

$\hat{\mu} = -0.3064$	$(\widehat{\alpha\beta})_{11} = -0.0310$	$(\widehat{\alpha\beta\gamma})_{11} = +0.0224$
$\hat{\alpha}_1 = +0.5066$	$(\widehat{\alpha\gamma})_{11} = +0.0311$	$(\widehat{\alpha\beta\delta})_{11} = +0.0719$
$\hat{\beta}_1 = +0.2426$	$(\widehat{\alpha\delta})_{11} = +0.2071$	$(\widehat{\alpha\gamma\delta})_{11} = +0.1404$
$\hat{\gamma}_1 = +0.2710$	$(\widehat{\beta\gamma})_{11} = -0.1126$	$(\widehat{\beta\gamma\delta})_{11} = -0.1252$
$\hat{\delta}_1 = +0.1700$	$(\widehat{\beta\delta})_{11} = +0.1285$	$(\widehat{\alpha\beta\gamma\delta})_{111} = +0.1289$
	$(\widehat{\gamma\delta})_{11} = -0.2888$	

In general, the estimated size of effect appears to decrease with the order of the interaction. The largest estimated effect on knowledge of cancer is reading newspapers. But, the information so far obtained provides no indication as to which effects are more plausible. Cox (1970, p.33) suggests a simple approximate technique, called the empirical logistic transform, for calculating tests of significance, which may be adapted to a likelihood analysis. The approximate variance of $\log(n_1/n_2)$ is $(n_1+n_2)/(n_1n_2)$. Since the maximum likelihood estimate of each parameter contains the $\log(n_1/n_2)$ from each cell, either as a sum or as a difference, the approximate variance of each estimate is the sum of the variances for the 16 cells divided by 16^2 as given in Table 3.11, (Cox suggests as a slightly better approximation $(n_1+n_2+1)(n_1+n_2+2)/$ $[(n_1+n_2)(n_1+1)(n_2+1)]$ which has been used here) *i.e.* $v = 0.0131$. Unfortunately, this approximation is only useful if $\hat{p}_1 = n_1/(n_1+n_2)$ is near 0.5 (say $0.3 < \hat{p}_1 < 0.7$) and if n_1+n_2 is large, both for each cell, which is not the case in the present example.

If the approximation is accurate, an approximate relative likelihood function, derived from the normal distribution (2.8), is for, say, α_1

$$R_A(\alpha_1) = \exp\left[-\frac{1}{2v}(\alpha_1 - \hat{\alpha}_1)^2\right] \tag{3.40}$$

and similarly for the other parameters. For these data, $\log R_A$ for α_1, β_1, γ_1, δ_1, equal to zero are -9.80, -2.25, -2.80, and -1.10 respectively. The approximate plausibility of each of the 16 parameters in the model being zero is directly related to the distance of the maximum likelihood estimate from zero. As will be seen in Section 4.2, this approximation is misleading for these data, primarily because many cells have very small counts.

All of the values of $\hat{p}_1$ must be close to 0.5 so that the corresponding binomial distributions are relatively symmetric, in agreement with the symmetry of the normal distribution. In addition, the number of observations in each cell should be large, increasingly so as $\hat{p}_1$ deviates from 0.5. If the procedure is applied to the questionnaire data of Table 3.6 with $0.035 < \hat{p}_1 < 0.250$ and $v = 0.0378$, the plausibility of difference in response according to experience is $\log R_A(\beta_1=0) = -4.07$, as compared with the exact value of -2.36 given in Table 3.7, a somewhat misleading result.

Lazarsfeld's data of Table 3.5 on listeners to classical music has

TABLE 3.12

Approximate (R_A, using the empirical logistic transform) and exact (R_B) likelihood analyses of the distribution of listeners to classical music given in Table 3.5.

	$\log R_A$	$\log R_B$	Number of parameters
Overall effect		-74.08	3
Difference in age	-1.61	-1.65	1
Difference in education	-41.63	-43.81	1
Interaction	-20.88	-23.22	1

$0.19 < \hat{p}_1 < 0.53$, but has at least 400 individuals per cell, so that the approximation will be good. For these data, $v = 0.0024$; the approximate and exact analyses are given in Table 3.12, showing the accuracy of the approximation.

This procedure is not, in general, applicable to the parameters corresponding to a polychotomous independent variable (including interaction parameters). If the observed values of the independent variable are ordered and metric, the model may be reparameterized using orthogonal polynomials in order to determine if the distribution of the response varies in a linear, quadratic, etc. manner as the value of the polychotomous independent variable changes. (The reparameterization may, of course, be applied to measure these effects whether or not the empirical logit transformation is to be used.) See Cox (1970, p.37) and Cochran and Cox (1966, p.62) for details about orthogonal polynomials. This procedure may be illustrated by application to the questionnaire data of Table 3.6 (although it is meaningless in this case, there being no metric among the sex—factory combinations). The estimated values for differences for sex—factory, as given in Section 3.4, are $\hat{\alpha}_1 = 0.393$, $\hat{\alpha}_2 = -0.350$, $\hat{\alpha}_3 = 0.623$, $\hat{\alpha}_4 = -0.666$ with zero sum so that only three parameters are independent. The reparameterization, using the orthogonal polynomials $(-3, -1, 1, 3)$, $(1, -1, -1, 1)$, and $(-1, 3, -3, 1)$ from Fisher and Yates (1963, p.98), yields first (linear), second (quadratic), and third-order main effects: $\hat{\phi}_1 = 4(-3\hat{\alpha}_1 - \hat{\alpha}_2 + \hat{\alpha}_3 + 3\hat{\alpha}_4) = -8.816$, $\hat{\phi}_2 = 4(\hat{\alpha}_1 - \hat{\alpha}_2 + \hat{\alpha}_3 - \hat{\alpha}_4) = 8.128$, and $\hat{\phi}_3 = 4(-\hat{\alpha}_1 + 3\hat{\alpha}_2 - 3\hat{\alpha}_3 + \hat{\alpha}_4) = -15.912$ respectively. This is equivalent to fitting a third degree polynomial regression as in Section 3.6. The estimate of the variance, v, now changes with each parameter, ϕ_i, according to the weighting. For example, for $\hat{\phi}_1$, v is the sum of $(-3)^2$ times the variances of all cells for men—factory 1, plus $(-1)^2$ times those of all cells for women—factory 1, plus etc. (see Cox, 1970, p.38). The same procedure may be applied to the interaction parameters. If the distances between observed values of the independent variable are unequal, Robson (1959) provides a simple method of calculating the orthogonal polynomials. The exact likelihood analysis may also be applied by replacing the α_i's by the ϕ_i's in the mathematical model and calculating maximum relative likelihoods.

The advantage of this empirical logistic transform as an approximation is the extremely limited number of calculations required to determine plausibility of the parameters. Unfortunately, it is only applicable in restricted circumstances. As well, it assumes that the

91

width of the likelihood graph is the same for all parameters, *i.e.* that the situation depicted in Fig. 3.3 does not occur, as it actually does with the data of Table 3.11 (see Section 4.2). In addition, the same procedure applied to the transformed parameter α_1' of eqn. (3.8) may yield different inferences since this type of approximation is not invariant, *i.e.* does not yield the same inference, under parameter transformation.

The procedure just outlined for determining plausibility of parameters being zero may be carried out with the aid only of a set of log tables. A slightly more tedious, but much more accurate procedure, not susceptible to extreme values of $\hat{p}_1$ but usually requiring a desk calculator, will be described in Section 4.2, since it is particularly useful with polychotomous response data. If resort to a computer is necessary, either because large quantities of data must be analyzed or because fewer parameters than cells are used (an unsaturated model) so that the maximum likelihood estimates cannot be obtained by solving linear equations, the estimation procedure of Appendix 2 will be used. Then, the negative of the diagonal elements of the inverse of the matrix of second derivatives, with the maximum likelihood estimates substituted in, are estimates of the variances of the parameters. This inverse matrix results automatically from the final step of the iteration procedure described in the appendix. These variance estimates will generally be a significant improvement on those (v) described above. They are used in the same way to yield approximate likelihood functions which are usually accurate with the linear logistic models described in this book. In many applications, this approximation will be sufficient to warrant the greatly reduced computer time. Kalbfleisch (1971, Chap.5) gives a description of this procedure in the one-parameter case.

The procedures of Sections 3.4 and 3.6 can be combined to form the analogue of normal theory covariance analysis. One possible application is to determine trend in the serial order of observations. Cox (1970, pp.70,93) analyzes artificial data comparing two treatments, A and B, tested in serial order in time; this analysis is reproduced in part here with data given in Table 3.13. The full model fitted is

$$\log\left[\frac{p_{ij1}}{p_{ij2}}\right] = \mu + \alpha_i + \beta_i(j-15) \qquad (i = 1,2; j = 1,...,30) \qquad (3.41)$$

where $\alpha_1 + \alpha_2 = 0$. The maximum likelihood estimates of the parameters of interest are $\hat{\alpha}_1 = -\hat{\alpha}_2 = -0.505$, $\hat{\beta}_1 = 0.139$, and $\hat{\beta}_2 =$

TABLE 3.13

Artificial data giving the comparison of dichotomous responses to two treatments (A and B) tested in serial order. Cox (1970, p.71).

Serial No.	Treatment	Response	Serial No.	Treatment	Response
1	B	0	16	A	1
2	A	0	17	A	0
3	B	1	18	B	0
4	A	1	19	B	1
5	B	0	20	A	1
6	B	0	21	A	1
7	A	0	22	A	1
8	A	1	23	B	1
9	B	0	24	B	0
10	B	1	25	A	1
11	A	1	26	A	1
12	B	0	27	B	1
13	B	1	28	A	1
14	A	1	29	B	1
15	A	0	30	B	1

TABLE 3.14

Exact likelihood analysis of the artificial data of Table 3.13 for serial trend in response under two treatments.

	$\log MR_B$	Number of parameters
Overall effect	−3.71	3
Between treatments ($\alpha_1 = \alpha_2 = 0; \beta_1 = \beta_2$)	−0.62	1
Trend ($\beta_1 = \beta_2 = 0$)	−3.02	1
Equal slope ($\beta_1 = \beta_2$)	−0.04	1

0.111. The likelihood analysis is given in Table 3.14, showing trend but not difference between treatments to be plausible. For the various submodels considered, the estimates of the remaining parameters change: equal slope, $\tilde{\alpha}_1 = -0.480$, $\tilde{\beta}_1 = \tilde{\beta}_2 = 0.121$; no trend, $\tilde{\alpha}_1 = -0.440$; and trend only, $\tilde{\beta}_1 = \tilde{\beta}_2 = 0.121$. This analysis provides a further example in which two maximized relative likelihood functions have very different graphs. The treatment parameter, α_1, is estimated to be much larger (farther from zero) than the regression parameters, β_i, but the data provide no evidence

93

that α_1 is not zero, whereas $\beta_i = 0$ is implausible, *i.e.* the linear trend is plausible but a difference between treatments is not. Of course, in this case, the units of measurement of the two parameters are different.

As can be seen from the preceding examples, these procedures can be adapted to a wide variety of special problems to obtain the required information from the data collected.

3.8 Departures from a Model

For dichotomous data, a statistical model describes the frequencies with which the two possible outcomes will be observed under various conditions defined by the independent variables. Occasionally, these frequencies are given by some theoretical model and the sociologist wishes to determine if the data collected support the model, *i.e.* if the observed and theoretical frequencies agree. Usually, a model is determined empirically from one or more sets of data and the sociologist wishes to determine if the same model explains adequately subsequent sets of data collected. This problem, in both its forms, was considered, for the simplest case, in the two examples of Section 2.5, but is immediately generalizable to more complex situations.

If the empirical or theoretical model does not adequately explain the observed frequencies, the sociologist will want to discover in what ways the new set of data departs from the previous model. Cox (1970, p.52) suggests a model to examine if the theoretical frequencies, p'_{ik}, are systematically too high or too low and too clustered or too dispersed

$$\log\left[\frac{p_{i1}}{p_{i2}}\right] = \alpha + \beta \log\left[\frac{p'_{i1}}{p'_{i2}}\right] \tag{3.42}$$

where p_{ik} is the population frequency to be estimated from the new sample and p'_{ik} the corresponding empirical or theoretical frequency. A value of the parameter α different from zero indicates high or low values of p'_{ik} and of β different from one, clustered or dispersed values. This model is exactly equivalent to the regression models (3.32) and (3.33); inferences about the plausibility of α being different from zero and β different from one are thus made using the procedures of Section 3.6.

If plausible departures from the hypothesized model are found,

94

the reasons will be sought for the differences between the observed data and the empirical or theoretical explanation. These reasons are then incorporated into the model; the theory is improved in order to explain these new results or the model is changed to explain both the previous empirical results and the new observations simultaneously. The values of the parameters α and β estimated will help to indicate what changes should be made.

CHAPTER 4

Polychotomous and
Multivariate Responses

4.1 Analysis of Multiple Responses

In many cases, dichotomizing responses before analysis as in the previous chapter involves considerable loss of information about the phenomenon under study. The various responses of a sample of individuals have been reduced into two opposing groups summarizing the divergences. This reduction may often be warranted, if the loss of information is not too significant, because of the greater ease of performing the required calculations. But when the loss of information becomes too great, a more complex analysis must be available. Polychotomous response variables were discussed in detail in Chapter 2 for situations where all individuals are sampled with all conditions affecting the response identical. The analysis of Chapter 3 will be extended in this chapter to cover such polychotomous responses when the conditions vary but when no other probability model than the multinomial is available.

Occasionally, several responses are measured simultaneously under various conditions and the sociologist wishes to determine how the changing conditions affect the responses simultaneously. For example, several questions are posed to samples of individuals from various social categories and the sociologist is interested in how the relationship among the responses to different questions changes with social category. This type of analysis is called multivariate. Relatively few new concepts are required in order to carry it out once the procedures for polychotomous responses have been elaborated.

With both polychotomous and multivariate response variables, the number of parameters in the statistical model is usually very large. The technique of maximizing the relative likelihood function over all parameters except one or two may introduce considerable approximation in these situations. Usually, only a small number of the parameters present are of direct interest, the others being considered to be "nuisance" parameters. Under certain special conditions, a conditional probability distribution will eliminate these nuisance parameters, allowing more precise inferences to be made about the parameters of interest. This approach will be discussed briefly in the last section of this chapter.

4.2 Inferences from Polychotomous Responses

Often, the response variable observed may take a number of different values instead of simply two: a dichotomous variable may involve a drastic reduction in information of some polychotomous variable. In Chapter 2, a method was discussed for reducing the number of values of a variable to be used in further analysis; other reduction procedures will be outlined in Chapter 5. Suppose now that a polychotomous variable is available, either naturally or by the reduction procedure, and that it takes more than two values (has more than two observed labels). This response variable is observed under a number of conditions or circumstances, and the sociologist wishes to determine how the distribution of the variable changes with the conditions.

This problem is much more complex than that previously considered because the probability distribution for a polychotomous variable is defined by $K-1$ parameters. Some way must be found to describe how all of these parameters change with the circumstances (with the independent variables). In most of the discussion in the previous chapter, the various possible values of all variables, response and independent, have only been assumed to be different, no restrictions of order or measure among the values having been required. This degree of generality will be useful in what follows.

But first, suppose that the polychotomous variable is a count or measure, such as the suicides in a town, the pupils in a school, the hours of work missed in a year, in the examples of Chapter 2. The procedures of Section 2.4 are applied and the probability distribution summarized by a plausible probability function with one or two parameters which describe the information in all $K-1$ parameters of the multinomial distribution. Only variation in these few parameters need be accounted for as the independent variables change. If the Poisson distribution has been found plausible, all of the analyses of the previous chapter may be carried out by explaining the variations in the parameter θ using mathematical models constructed from eqn. (1.20).

A very large part of classical statistical analysis is based on this procedure by assuming that the distribution of the polychotomous response variable may be represented by a normal distribution (2.7). Since this distribution has two parameters, the variance parameter, θ_2, is assumed to remain constant for all values of the independent variables, and mathematical models are constructed to explain variation in the mean parameter, θ_1. Analyses using the normal distribution are well documented, both in the statistical literature and elsewhere, and will not be discussed here. And, unfortunately, consideration of the appropriate analysis when some other probability function, such as the Poisson, is assumed, is beyond the scope of this book. Attention will be restricted to polychotomous response data with no necessary assumption of order or measure.

If the multinomial distribution cannot be summarized by a single parameter in a probability function, changes in the distribution cannot be so summarized. But, the plausibility of an effect of an independent variable can be obtained, as with the third example of Section 3.4. Since large numbers of parameters are involved when all variables are polychotomous, and since large changes in the number of parameters in a model often involve very small relative likelihoods while still giving plausible models, the use of differences in log likelihoods (log relative likelihoods) instead of ratios of likelihoods (relative likelihoods) is convenient.

In the simplest case, a polychotomous response variable, Y, depends on one polychotomous independent variable, X_1. The probability of the value y_{ik} being observed under condition x_{1i} is p_{ik} so that the log relative likelihood function is

$$\log R_M(p_{ik}) = \sum_i \sum_k n_{ik} (\log p_{ik} - \log \hat{p}_{ik}) \tag{4.1}$$

Comparison shows that this is the logarithm of the relative likelihood function given in eqn. (1.15). If the response is independent of the condition, p_{ik} will not vary with X_1 but will be constant, $p_{ik} = p_k$ (all k) for every value x_{1i}. Since the maximum likelihood estimates are $\hat{p}_{ik} = n_{ik}/n_i$ and $\hat{p}_k = n_{.k}/n_{..}$, the plausibility of the independence model is given by

$$\log R_M(p_{ik} = \hat{p}_k) = \sum_i \sum_k n_{ik} \log (n_{i.} n_{.k}/n_{ik} n_{..}) \quad (4.2)$$

which, again, is the logarithm of eqn. (1.16). Since this expression is symmetric in the two variables, the choice of which variable is the response (dependent) does not affect the measure of plausible independence (see Section 4.4). This may be expected from eqns. (3.28) and (3.29), since for independence the two variables are symmetric. Thus, eqn. (4.2) provides a measure of plausibility of the independence of two variables jointly distributed, as measured in an $I \times K$ table of counts (contingency table).

If independence is found to be implausible, other relationships among the distributions for different values of X_1 may be considered. Suppose, for example, that the sociologist hypothesizes that values x_{13} and x_{14} provide the same effect, x_{15}, x_{16}, and x_{17} another identical effect, etc. This implies that $p_{3k} = p_{4k}$ and $p_{5k} = p_{6k} = p_{7k}$ (all k). If these relationships are substituted into the relative likelihood function (4.1) and the maximum likelihood estimates obtained, the plausibility of this model may be determined.

When more than one independent variable is present, additional problems arise, since interaction among the variables must be accounted for. Since this is a complex problem, discussed in the next section, a good approximation will be used here, obtained by analogy with the analysis of Section 3.4 and with normal theory analysis of variance (see Lindsey and Nash, 1972).

Consider the case with two independent variables, X_1 and X_2. Call the likelihood function for the overall model, including interactions, and with maximum likelihood estimates substituted in, L_{IJ} as defined by

$$\log L_{IJ} = \sum_i \sum_j \sum_k n_{ijk} \log (n_{ijk}/n_{ij.}) \quad (4.3)$$

Then, L_{IJ} is simply the denominator of the relative likelihood function

$$\log R_M(p_{ijk}) = \sum_i \sum_j \sum_k n_{ijk} (\log p_{ijk} - \log \hat{p}_{ijk}) \quad (4.4)$$

with $\hat{p}_{ijk} = n_{ijk}/n_{ij.}$.

Logically, the effect of interaction between X_1 and X_2 is usually considered first. But, since this is complex, suppose that the hypothesis is made that the response Y is completely independent of X_1. Then, $p_{ijk} = p_{jk}$ (all j,k), $\hat{p}_{jk} = n_{.jk}/n_{.j.}$ and the maximized log likelihood function is

$$\log L_J = \sum_i \sum_j \sum_k n_{ijk} \log(n_{.jk}/n_{.j.})\qquad(4.5)$$

so that the log maximum relative likelihood giving the plausibility of the distribution of Y being independent of X_1 is

$$\log R_M(p_{ijk} = \hat{p}_{jk}) = \log L_J - \log L_{IJ}$$

$$= \sum_i \sum_j \sum_k n_{ijk} \log(n_{.jk} n_{ij.}/n_{.j.} n_{ijk})\qquad(4.6)$$

Similarly, if Y is hypothesized to be independent of X_2, $p_{ijk} = p_{ik}$ (all i,k), $\hat{p}_{ik} = n_{i.k}/n_{i..}$, the maximized log likelihood function is

$$\log L_I = \sum_i \sum_j \sum_k n_{ijk} \log(n_{i.k}/n_{i..})\qquad(4.7)$$

and the log maximum relative likelihood

$$\log R_M(p_{ijk} = \hat{p}_{ik}) = \log L_I - \log L_{IJ}$$

$$= \sum_i \sum_j \sum_k n_{ijk} \log(n_{i.k} n_{ij.}/n_{i..} n_{ijk})\qquad(4.8)$$

If the response is independent of both X_1 and X_2, $p_{ijk} = p_k$ (all k), $\hat{p}_k = n_{..k}/n_{...}$, the maximized log likelihood function is

$$\log L = \sum_i \sum_j \sum_k n_{ijk} \log(n_{..k}/n_{...})\qquad(4.9)$$

and the log maximum relative likelihood

$$\log R_M(p_{ijk} = \hat{p}_k) = \log L - \log L_{IJ}$$

$$= \sum_i \sum_j \sum_k n_{ijk} \log(n_{..k} n_{ij.}/n_{...} n_{ijk})\qquad(4.10)$$

All of these measures of plausibility, eqns. (4.6), (4.8), and (4.10), are exact for determining the independence stated in each case. Each is obtained by eliminating both the direct effect of the independent variable(s) and the interaction.

By analogy with normal theory, an approximate measure of the

100

plausibility of interaction between the variables X_1 and X_2 is given by

$$\log R_M(\text{no interaction}) \doteq \log L_I + \log L_J - \log L - \log L_{IJ} \quad (4.11)$$

If the interaction effect is not found to be implausible, the sociologist will want to determine the plausibility of effect of each of the variables X_1 and X_2 without eliminating the interaction, as was done in relative likelihood functions (4.6) and (4.8). This is equivalent to mathematical models (3.19) and (3.20) for the case of a dichotomous response. Again, an approximate measure may be used. The plausibility of no effect of X_1 in the presence of an interaction effect is

$$\log R_M(\text{interaction but not } X_1) \doteq \log L - \log L_I \quad (4.12)$$

and correspondingly of X_2 is

$$\log R_M(\text{interaction but not } X_2) \doteq \log L - \log L_J \quad (4.13)$$

These approximations, in effect, assume that the likelihood function factors, so that the terms containing parameters not of interest cancel (see Section 4.5).

To recapitulate, for a polychotomous response with two independent variables, the approximate plausibility of an interaction between X_1 and X_2 is determined using eqn. (4.11). If an interaction is implausible, eqns. (4.6) and (4.8) are used to determine the exact plausibilities of the independence of Y from X_1 and X_2 respectively. If an interaction is plausible, eqns. (4.12) and (4.13) give the approximate plausibilities of no effect of X_1 and of X_2 respectively, in the presence of an interaction effect.

Data with more than two independent variables with all variables polychotomous will not often be met in practice, since the very large number of parameters requires a sample containing an extremely large number of individuals in order that most of the cells of the table be non-zero. If the relative likelihoods are required, they may be derived, as in this case, by analogy with normal theory analysis of variance; see the last example of this section.

With these procedures available, the reader is now able to analyze systems of dependence of the form of eqn. (3.27), or more complex, in which any of the variables may be polychotomous. Since this analysis is straightforward, being similar to that for dichotomous variables given in Sections 3.4 and 3.5, and since such an analysis is very space-consuming, no numerical example will be given here.

Instead, examples of two other uses of the analysis of polychotomous data will be given. Suppose that the sociologist is deriving an index to distinguish differences between towns. He has constructed two indices which are relatively easy to use and has available a third for a limited number of towns which is expensive to apply, but which he knows to be accurate. He wants to discover if either of the simpler indices reproduces sufficiently well the complex index. Suppose that the indices are the values x_{11}, x_{12}, and x_{13} of the independent variable X_1. Each index counts the numbers of individuals in 26 different status groups (Y) present in a town, with each index using a different method of obtaining the counts (2 methods of polling and census data). The sociologist applies the three methods to twenty towns which he knows to be different, labelled by the values of the independent variable X_2.

Since interest lies in comparison of the indices in pairs, three separate analyses may be performed, each being dichotomous in X_1, but with Y taking 26 values and X_2 20. From the relative likelihoods (4.10)—(4.13) derived above, the results of the analysis are given in Table 4.1. Although all of the relative likelihoods are extremely small, some information can be obtained from the data. Since it is known that these towns should be different, the effects between towns may be considered to be plausible in the table.

The total number of parameters in the full model, for comparison between two indices, is $2 \times 20 \times (26-1) = 1000$. With no effect between towns but assuming an interaction, using eqn. (4.12), the reduction in parameter number is $(20-1)(26-1) = 475$. With no difference in indices but with interaction, the reduction is

TABLE 4.1

Approximate likelihood analysis of data for the comparison of two indices (1,2) with a control (3) to determine which gives the more accurate measure of difference among towns.

Indices compared	log MR_M			Number of parameters
	3 vs. 1	3 vs. 2	1 vs. 2	
Overall effect	−5931.76	−3054.20	−4522.65	975
Between towns	−1430.41	−1474.20	−1840.90	475
Between indices	−3748.50	−457.93	−2670.17	25
Interaction	−752.84	−1122.08	−11.58	475

$(2-1)(26-1) = 25$. The reduction in number of parameters with elimination of the interaction is $(20-1)(2-1)(26-1) = 475$.

For equal levels of plausibility, the relative likelihood of no difference between towns, with 475 parameters eliminated, would be expected to be much smaller than that for differences between indices, with 25 parameters eliminated, and equal to that for interaction, also with 475 parameters eliminated. Since the differences between towns are known to be plausible, this implies that a difference between indices 3 (the control) and 1 and between 1 and 2 is very plausible. Index 2 is much closer to the control index 3, but also seems to show a plausible difference. The data should now be inspected to attempt to determine the reasons for these differences. For example, the two simple indices may count different subsets of the 26 status groups well.

As another example, suppose that for 10 age groups (X_1), workers in six similar factories (X_2) are classified according to their (48) jobs (Y). The sociologist knows that the job distribution varies with age in the factories and wants to determine if the samples from the six factories may be combined without losing the change in job distribution according to age. With the same procedures as in the previous example, the results are given in Table 4.2.

When very large changes in the numbers of parameters occur, some rough measure to determine plausibility is convenient. If the number ν of parameters eliminated is greater than $-2 \log R$, one may assume that the model is rather plausible. If the number ν is such that $(-4 \log R)^{\frac{1}{2}} - (2\nu - 1)^{\frac{1}{2}}$ is greater than 2 or 3, the model may be considered implausible. In between these two limits, the inferences are uncertain. With these criteria, the models with no difference among factories and with no interaction are plausible,

TABLE 4.2

Approximate likelihood analysis of data on the job distribution of workers in ten age groups to determine if the samples from six factories may be combined.

	$\log MR_M$	Number of parameters
Overall effect	-301.65	2773
Between ages	-263.43	423
Between factories	-22.82	235
Interaction	-15.40	2115

TABLE 4.3

Approximate likelihood analysis of the questionnaire data of Table 3.6 to be compared with the exact analysis of Table 3.7.

	$\log MR_B$		Number of parameters
	No interaction	Interaction	
Overall effect		−7.57	7
Between sex—factories	−4.05	−3.66	3
Between experiences	−3.91	−3.51	1
Interaction		−0.39	3

whereas that with no differences between ages is implausible, *i.e.* the effects of interaction and between factories are implausible and the effects between ages are plausible so that the samples may be combined. And in the previous example, from Table 4.1, the differences between indices 2 and 3 are also plausible.

The procedures of this section may also be applied to dichotomous response variables in order to reduce the amount of calculation required. Consideration of a number of the examples of Chapter 3 in this light is useful to provide some idea of the magnitude of the approximation involved. The analysis for the questionnaire data of Table 3.6 and for the data on babies crying of Table 3.8 are given in Tables 4.3 and 4.4 respectively. These analyses may be compared with those of Tables 3.7 and 3.9. Remember that with the approximate method, the no-interaction analysis assumes the plausibility of no interaction to be unity; if this is not so, the interaction effect will be included in *each* of the main effects using the no-interaction model. In the second ex-

TABLE 4.4

Approximate likelihood analysis of the data on babies crying of Table 3.8 to be compared with the exact analysis of Table 3.9.

	$\log MR_B$		Number of parameters
	No interaction	Interaction	
Overall effect		−23.23	35
Rocking	−10.49	−1.80	1
Between days	−21.43	−12.75	17
Interaction		−8.69	17

104

TABLE 4.5

Approximate likelihood analysis of the data on listeners to classical music of Table 3.5 to be compared with the previous approximate analysis using the empirical logistic transform and the exact analysis, both given in Table 3.12.

	$\log MR_B$	Number of parameters
Overall effect	−74.08	3
Difference in age	−0.18	1
Difference in education	−47.96	1
Interaction	−25.93	1

ample, interaction is plausible and the plausibilities for the two main effects in the no-interaction analysis are correspondingly inflated. Otherwise, the approximate analysis shows no great difference from the exact analysis of the previous chapter.

The data on listeners to classical music may also be analyzed in this way, as given in Table 4.5. The very plausible effects are of education and of interaction between age and education. This ordering is the same as that for the sizes of the parameter estimates given in Section 3.4, but emphasizes the role of education on listener preference. This analysis, when compared with those of Section 3.7 as summarized in Table 3.12, can be seen to be about as different from the exact analysis as the empirical logistic approximation.

The advantages of the analysis of this section are that many fewer calculations are required than for the exact analysis of Section 3.4 (instead of an electronic computer, log tables for the three examples just considered; in addition, a desk calculator for the next), while the limitations of the empirical logistic procedure of Section 3.7 are avoided.

The data on knowledge of cancer given in Table 3.11 may also be analyzed in this way. Indeed, with such complex data, an approximate method such as this is recommended, even using a computer, to determine if sufficient information can be gained from the data or if the exact time-consuming analysis of Section 3.4 must be applied. In the previous three examples with a dichotomous response, the likelihoods of this section could be used directly. But here four independent variables are present and the situation is more complex. With two independent variables and four types of parameters, four log likelihoods were calculated: log L, log L_I, log L_J, and log L_{IJ}. With 16 (types of) parameters in eqn. (3.39), 16 log likelihoods must be calculated. For example,

$$\log L_{\text{ABC}} = \sum_i \sum_j \sum_l \sum_m \sum_k n_{ijlmk} \log(n_{ijl.k}/n_{ijl..})$$

These are combined as previously to give the log maximum relative likelihoods, *e.g.* main effect of A with interaction: $\log L - \log L_{\text{A}}$; without interaction: $\log L_{\text{BCD}} - \log L_{\text{ABCD}}$; second-order interaction ABC: $\log L - \log L_{\text{A}} - \log L_{\text{B}} - \log L_{\text{C}} + \log L_{\text{AB}} + \log L_{\text{AC}} + \log L_{\text{BC}} - \log L_{\text{ABC}}$; etc. The results are given in Table 4.6. A number of other analyses can be easily calculated assuming that only some of the interactions are zero, *e.g.* second-order interaction ABC assuming the third-order interaction ABCD to be zero: $\log L_{\text{D}} - \log L_{\text{AD}} - \log L_{\text{BD}} - \log L_{\text{CD}} + \log L_{\text{ABD}} + \log L_{\text{ACD}} + \log L_{\text{BCD}} - \log L_{\text{ABCD}}$. For this example, these analyses confirm the results given in Table 4.6.

Some care must be used in interpreting the results in a complex

TABLE 4.6

Approximate likelihood analysis of the data on knowledge of cancer given in Table 3.11.

		$\log MR_B$		Number of parameters
		No interaction	*Interaction*	
Overall effect			−108.13	15
Main effects	A	−19.98	−52.89	1
	B	−4.60	−12.12	1
	C	−45.25	−75.23	1
	D	−7.65	−8.58	1
First-order interactions	AB		+7.63	1
	AC		+31.41	1
	AD		+3.12	1
	BC		+4.80	1
	BD		+1.69	1
	CD		+2.37	1
Second-order interactions	ABC		−4.08	1
	ABD		−1.74	1
	ACD		−3.74	1
	BCD		−1.08	1
Third-order interaction	ABCD		+0.30	1

example such as this. The plausibility of overall effect, which is an exact measure, is great. The plausibilities given in the no-interaction analysis are exact if each is considered to measure not only the main effect, say A, but also all interactions containing A, thus with a large amount of overlap. In this example, main effects A and C, plus all interactions containing either, and especially both, of these two effects are most plausible. Next, the plausibilities of those interactions containing both A and C should be considered. Since plausibilities of all interactions are calculated approximately, the results may give positive log relative likelihoods if the exact plausibility of no interaction is very large (close to one or log close to zero). All of the first-order interactions appear to have high plausibility of being zero. The two second-order interactions, ABC and ACD, containing both A and C have relatively low plausibility of being zero. Thus, this approximate analysis indicates that the exposure to newspapers, (A), and to solid reading, (C), and the interaction of these two combined with exposure to radio, (B), or to lectures, (D), have the most plausible effects on knowledge of cancer.

These inferences from the data cannot be derived from simple inspection of the parameter estimates given in Section 3.7. For some estimates far from zero, the data provide little evidence that they might not be zero, whereas for others closer to zero, the data indicate much greater implausibility of their being zero (the situation of Fig. 3.3). Thus, $(\hat{\gamma\delta})_{11} = -0.29$ is about as far from zero as $\hat{\gamma}_1 = 0.27$ but could much more plausibly be zero.

This approximate analysis does not exclude the possibility that exposure to radio and to lectures have plausible influences on knowledge of cancer. The exact analysis would be required to determine this with certainty. But, the analysis given has separated out the most influential factors with a minimum of time-consuming calculations.

4.3 Mathematical Models for Polychotomous Responses

With a dichotomous response, the variation of only the one parameter of the binomial distribution need be described as the conditions change. For a polychotomous response variable, with K possible outcomes, the multinomial distribution contains $K-1$ independent parameters. Thus, $K-1$ independent equations must be constructed in the mathematical model to describe the change in the distribution of responses as the conditions (independent variables) change. Since the multinomial distribution contains K parameters, one must be eliminated. The simplest way to do this, while still retaining symmetry, is to relate each parameter p_k to the geometric mean $\dot{p}$ of the K parameters. An equation is constructed describing the function

$$\log(p_k/\dot{p}) = \log p_k - \frac{1}{K}\sum_k \log p_k.$$
(4.14)

for each of the K parameters. Since the K equations will sum to zero, only $K-1$ are independent as required.

Suppose that two independent variables are available. The model, analogous to eqn. (3.15) for dichotomous data, is

$$\log(p_{ijk}/\dot{p}_{ij}) = \mu_k + \alpha_{ik} + \beta_{jk} + \gamma_{ijk}$$
(4.15)

where

$$\sum_k \mu_k = \sum_i \alpha_{ik} = \sum_k \alpha_{ik} = \sum_j \beta_{jk} = \sum_k \beta_{jk} = \sum_i \gamma_{ijk} = \sum_j \gamma_{ijk} =$$

$$\sum_k \gamma_{ijk} = 0$$

For each value of k, the maximum likelihood estimate of eqn. (4.14) is calculated under each combination (i,j) of values of the independent variables. Since the model (4.15) contains as many independent parameters as does the multinomial distribution (the model is saturated), the maximum likelihood estimates for each k are obtained by solving linear equations in the same way as for the corresponding dichotomous model. The summations over k in the constraints will automatically be fulfilled.

The model may be rewritten in terms of the parameters p_{ijk}.

$$p_{ijk} = \frac{\exp(\mu_k + \alpha_{ik} + \beta_{jk} + \gamma_{ijk})}{\sum_k \exp(\mu_k + \alpha_{ik} + \beta_{jk} + \gamma_{ijk})}$$
(4.16)

for substitution into the multinomial relative likelihood function (4.4). Inferences are made about certain parameters maximizing over the others. For example, eqn. (4.6) is the exact log maximum relative likelihood for the model with $\alpha_{ik} = \gamma_{ijk} = 0$ (all i,j,k), eqn. (4.12) is the approximate likelihood with $\alpha_{ik} = 0$ (all i,k), and

108

TABLE 4.7

Observed distribution of votes in four successive French elections in two voting districts. Abstentions include all those registered in the district in the year but not voting. The number registered in a district varies from year to year.

	Abstention	Communist party	Left non-communist	Gaullist	Right non-Gaullist
District 1					
1958	851	156	223	324	1376
1962	1043	151	217	441	989
1967	743	154	261	734	790
1968	650	182	450	1158	208
District 2					
1958	1369	92	239	1522	1856
1962	1489	114	238	2003	1175
1967	905	118	318	2411	1088
1968	931	120	528	2811	412

eqn. (4.11) the approximate likelihood with $\gamma_{ijk} = 0$ (all i,j,k). The exact maximum relative likelihoods with certain parameters fixed (often at zero) may be obtained in the same way as for the dichotomous response variables in Chapter 3, but the process is very time-consuming since many more parameters remain for which estimates must be obtained from non-linear equations (see Appendix 2).

The analysis of data with a polychotomous response is thus the same as with a dichotomous response except that the mathematical model contains more than one equation. In fact, this procedure reduces to that for the dichotomous responses of Chapter 3 when $K = 2$.

One application of this analysis is to election results. Table 4.7 gives the returns for four elections in France in two voting districts (communes). The results have been grouped into five categories ($K = 5$). The two independent variables are the year ($I = 4$) and the district ($J = 2$). The values of eqn. (4.14) are calculated for each cell, e.g. 0.704 for abstentions in 1958 in the first district, yielding another 8×5 table. Equation (4.15) is applied to each column (type of vote) and the linear equations solved to give the maximum likelihood estimates of the parameters, as shown in Table 4.8. From these estimates, certain inferences are immediate. From $\hat{\mu}_k$, abstentions and right votes are above average in number

TABLE 4.8

Maximum likelihood estimates of the parameters of the multinomial mathematical model (4.15) for the data on French elections given in Table 4.7.

k	1	2	3	4	5
$\hat{\mu}_k$	+0.633	−1.346	−0.557	+0.787	+0.482
$\hat{\alpha}_{1k}$	+0.122	−0.097	−0.231	−0.461	+0.667
$\hat{\alpha}_{2k}$	+0.243	−0.030	−0.270	−0.193	+0.249
$\hat{\alpha}_{3k}$	−0.185	−0.011	−0.041	+0.146	+0.090
$\hat{\alpha}_{4k}$	−0.181	+0.138	+0.542	+0.508	−1.006
$\hat{\beta}_{1k}$	+0.002	+0.362	+0.111	−0.467	−0.009
$\hat{\gamma}_{1k}$	−0.054	+0.089	+0.041	−0.120	+0.046
$\hat{\gamma}_{2k}$	+0.005	−0.036	+0.028	−0.105	+0.108
$\hat{\gamma}_{3k}$	+0.063	−0.065	−0.046	+0.036	+0.012
$\hat{\gamma}_{4k}$	−0.015	+0.013	−0.024	+0.190	−0.166

(average being 1/5 of registered voters) and left votes below. From $\hat{\alpha}_{ik}$, the left and Gaullist votes tend to grow and the abstentions decline over the four years with marked changes in 1968. From $\hat{\beta}_{1k}$, the first district tends to vote further left than the second, with little difference in abstentions and in right non-Gaullist votes. Most of the interaction estimates are small, except in the right votes which may require further analysis.

This initial analysis provides no indication if other inferences opposed to those stated are almost as plausible. The first step towards this objective is to apply the analysis of the previous section (requiring log tables and desk calculator). The results are

TABLE 4.9

Approximate likelihood analysis of the data for the French elections given in Table 4.7.

	$\log MR_M$		Number of parameters
	No interaction	Interaction	
Overall effect		−2509.31	28
Between years	−1750.14	−1705.70	12
Between districts	−803.51	−759.18	4
Interaction		−44.44	12

110

summarized in Table 4.9. All of the effects are very plausible according to this approximate analysis, although the interaction is much less so than the others. This result does not imply that all of the parameters individually have very low plausibility of being zero, but only that, for example, all of the β_{jk}'s cannot be eliminated simultaneously. Further analysis is required to determine if β_{11} and β_{15} might plausibly be zero. An exact analysis using eqn. (4.16) in the likelihood function will answer such questions.

Since a trend over years has been noted, the analysis given for the second example of Section 3.7 may usefully be applied. Equation (3.41) may be adapted to this requirement.

$$\log(p_{ijk}/\overset{\bullet}{p}_{ij}) = \mu_k + \alpha_{jk}(i-1963) + \beta_{jk} \tag{4.17}$$

where

$$\sum_k \mu_k = 0, \quad \sum_k \alpha_{jk} = 0, \quad \sum_j \beta_{jk} = \sum_k \beta_{jk} = 0$$

The linear effect of the interaction parameter γ_{ijk} of eqn. (4.15) is incorporated into α_{jk}, hence the lack of constraint summing over j. The value 1963 is chosen for ease of computation only. Because of the change of voting pattern in 1968, a quadratic term, say $\gamma_{jk}(i-1963)^2$, will probably be required to explain the trend adequately. (If the third-order term, say $\phi_{jk}(i-1963)^3$, is also added, the model becomes exactly equivalent to eqn. (4.15), since the highest order is one less than the number of variable values; see Section 3.7). The fitting of orthogonal polynomials, also discussed in Section 3.7, is an equivalent approach to this analysis, but these must be calculated since the distance (time) between years is unequal.

The parameter estimates given in Table 4.8 describe exactly the voting phenomenon observed in the two districts for the four years since Table 4.7 contains all and not a sample of the votes. The question of inferences about parameter values is not relevant in this context. If these districts are considered as representative of certain other districts in France, the inferences about parameter values apply to the overall population of such districts. Likewise, the inferences might apply with respect to other years. In either case, other independent variables will usually be required for an adequate explanation. The application of a likelihood analysis (Table 4.9) to such data for all the districts of France does not

111

make sense (except in attempts to predict the results of a future election, etc.) since no hypothetical superpopulation presents itself (except other years). The parameter values, as given in Table 4.8, may, of course, be calculated, but these are exact. Likelihood inferences are applied when only partial information about (a sample from) a population of individuals is available, in order to see what can be said about the overall population.

If the registered voters could be divided into 5^4 groups of individuals according to their voting pattern over the four elections, or even into 3×5^2 groups according to their change in voting behaviour between successive elections, perhaps using some sampling technique, a time series analysis, such as that outlined in Chapter 6 for social mobility, could be applied. In this way, the pattern of change in voting behaviour could be incorporated into the statistical model as a stochastic process.

4.4 Multivariate Data

When a survey has recorded a number of different types of responses, perhaps as answers to several questions, the sociologist may wish to determine how the distributions of responses vary simultaneously. The statistical models required for this analysis are not fundamentally different from those for polychotomous responses described in the previous section. If two types of response are recorded with K and L possible outcomes respectively, this is equivalent to a polychotomous response with KL outcomes. For example, with two yes/no questions, possible outcomes are no/no, no/yes, yes/no, and yes/yes. But, more complex (probability) models may be developed relating outcomes of the various response variables.

Consider multivariate responses within one homogeneous group of individuals. A probability model may be constructed among outcomes for the response variables observed. The multivariate equivalent to eqn. (4.14) is used as a basis for the analysis. For two response variables, this becomes

$$\log(q_{ik}/\dot{q}) = \log q_{ik} - \frac{1}{IK} \sum_i \sum_k \log q_{ik} \qquad (4.18)$$

with $\Sigma\Sigma q_{ik} = 1$. Since this relationship is not conditional on the circumstances, q is used instead of p. The probability model describes how the proportions of outcomes for the two responses change simultaneously

$$\log(q_{ik}/\dot{q}) = \lambda_i + \rho_k + \psi_{ik} \tag{4.19}$$

where

$$\sum_i \lambda_i = \sum_k \rho_k = \sum_i \psi_{ik} = \sum_k \psi_{ik} = 0$$

Since the sum over all values of eqn. (4.18) is zero, no mean parameter, analogous to μ in the mathematical models, appears in the probability model (4.19). The parameters λ_i and ρ_k describe how the frequencies of response change with the outcome for each response variable. These parameters are related to the marginal distributions, $q_{i.}$ and $q_{.k}$ of Section 3.3. But, the parameters of most interest are ψ_{ik} since they describe the interdependence of the two response variables.

When $\psi_{ik} = 0$ (all i,k), the two response variables (i,k) are marginally independent and

$$q_{ik} = q_{i.} q_{.k} \qquad \text{(all } i,k) \tag{4.20}$$

For two variables, marginal independence is equivalent to the conditional independence, $\alpha_i = 0$ (all i) in eqn. (3.7), between a response and one independent variable of Section 3.2

$$p_{ik} = p_k \qquad \text{or} \qquad q_{ik} = q_{i.} q_{.k}/q_{..} \tag{4.21}$$

(with $p_{ik} = q_{ik}/q_{i.}$, $p_k = q_{.k}/q_{..}$; see Section 3.3) since $q_{..} = 1$.

In order to make inferences about the parameters, eqn. (4.19) may be solved for the proportions

$$q_{ik} = \frac{\exp(\lambda_i + \rho_k + \psi_{ik})}{\sum_i \sum_k \exp(\lambda_i + \rho_k + \psi_{ik})} \tag{4.22}$$

and substituted into the bivariate multinomial relative likelihood function

$$R_{BM}(\lambda_i, \rho_k, \psi_{ik}) = \tag{4.23}$$

$$\left[\sum_i \sum_k \exp(\lambda_i + \rho_k + \psi_{ik}) \right]^{-n_{..}} \prod_i \prod_k \left[\frac{\exp(\lambda_i + \rho_k + \psi_{ik})}{\hat{q}_{ik}} \right]^{n_{ik}}$$

derived from the multinomial extension of eqn. (3.10). With two

113

variables, inferences about the marginal independence, as measured by the parameter ψ_{ik}, are the same as those for conditional independence, as measured by α_{ik} from the polychotomous equivalent of eqn. (3.7), *i.e.* the maximum relative likelihood functions for α_{ik} and for ψ_{ik} are identical. The maximum likelihood estimates are

$$\hat{\alpha}_{ik} = \hat{\psi}_{ik} = \log n_{ik} - \frac{1}{K} \sum_k \log n_{ik} - \frac{1}{I} \sum_i \log n_{ik} +$$

$$\frac{1}{IK} \sum_i \sum_k \log n_{ik} \qquad (4.24)$$

and the plausibility of $\alpha_{ik} = 0$ or of $\psi_{ik} = 0$ (all i,k) is given by eqn. (4.2).

With more than two response variables (multivariate multinomial distribution), the situation becomes more complex. With three variables, eqn. (4.19) becomes

$$\log(q_{ijk}/\dot{q}) = \lambda_i + \rho_j + \kappa_k + \psi_{ij} + \eta_{ik} + \xi_{jk} + \tau_{ijk} \qquad (4.25)$$

Here, two types of marginal independence are present. If $\psi_{ij} = \eta_{ik} = \xi_{jk} = \tau_{ijk} = 0$ (all i,j,k), the three variables (i,j,k) have complete marginal independence with

$$q_{ijk} = q_{i..} q_{.j.} q_{..k} \qquad (4.26)$$

If, say, $\eta_{ik} = \xi_{jk} = \tau_{ijk} = 0$ (all i,j,k), the first two variables (i,j) are jointly independent of the third (k) with

$$q_{ijk} = q_{ij.} q_{..k} \qquad (4.27)$$

etc. As with two response variables, inferences are made about plausibility of these various types of independence.

These measures of marginal independence may be compared with the conditional independence of Sections 3.4 and 4.3. Parameters with the same subscripts in models (4.15) and (4.25) will be seen below to be identical. If $\alpha_{ik} = \beta_{jk} = \gamma_{ijk} = 0$ (all i,j,k) in eqn. (4.15) or equivalently, eqn. (3.17) holds, the response variable (k) is conditionally independent of the two independent variables (i,j) as expressed by

$$p_{ijk} = p_k \quad \text{or} \quad q_{ijk} = q_{ij.} q_{..k}/q_{...} \qquad (4.28)$$

Since $q_{...} = 1$, this is identical to eqn. (4.27) for the joint marginal independence of two variables from a third. If $\beta_{jk} = \gamma_{ijk} = 0$ (or

114

$\xi_{jk} = \tau_{ijk} = 0$; all i,j,k), the variables j and k are conditionally (or marginally) independent of each other, but dependent on i

$$p_{ijk} = p_{ik} \quad \text{or} \quad q_{ijk} = q_{i.k}q_{ij.}/q_{i..} \qquad (4.29)$$

If only $\gamma_{ijk} = 0$ (or $\tau_{ijk} = 0$; all i,j,k), the response (k) depends conditionally on the two variables (i,j), independently of each other, or the three variables are pairwise dependent, as expressed by

$$p_{ijk} = p_{ik}p_{jk}/p_k \quad \text{or} \quad q_{ijk} = q_{ij.}q_{i.k}q_{.jk}q_{...}/q_{i..}q_{.j.}q_{..k} \qquad (4.30)$$

This is a necessary but not sufficient condition for the stated independence, since the sum over k of p_{ijk} must be unity (all i,j).

When a multivariate response varies with the conditions, the initial analysis of the data is identical to that described in Sections 4.2 and 4.3 for polychotomous responses, but with additional subscripts added for the dependent variables. With two independent variables, the q's in eqn. (4.18) for each cell become p's and eqn. (4.15) becomes

$$\log(p_{ijkl}/\dot{p}_{ij}) = \mu_{kl} + \alpha_{ikl} + \beta_{jkl} + \gamma_{ijkl} \qquad (4.31)$$

where

$$\sum_k \sum_l \mu_{kl} = 0, \quad \sum_i \alpha_{ikl} = \sum_k \sum_l \alpha_{ikl} = 0, \text{ etc.}$$

Inferences about changes in the simultaneous (multivariate) distribution of the responses to, say, two questions, as the two independent variables change, are made as previously described for polychotomous responses. An example of such data, with two yes/no questions posed to individuals in four age groups in three different cities is given in Table 4.10, from medical data of Grizzle and Williams (1972).

This elementary (polychotomous response) analysis will reveal if and how the multivariate distribution of the responses changes with the conditions. But it does not demonstrate how the relationship among the responses changes. An important part of the information in the data has been neglected. For example, the sociologist may wish to determine how the dependence of the two responses on each other varies. With several polychotomous responses, this involves a number of parameters in each cell (for example, from eqn. (4.19), for two response variables the $(K-1)(L-1)$ parameters $\psi_{kl})$ which is less than the number $(KL-1)$ of parameters in eqn. (4.18). For the bivariate dichoto-

TABLE 4.10

The observed bivariate distribution of responses to two questions, divided according to city and age group. Grizzle and Williams (1972).

Age group	Question 1	Question 2					
		City 1		City 2		City 3	
		No	Yes	No	Yes	No	Yes
35—44	No	9	8	7	3	4	7
	Yes	6	6	2	5	2	3
45—54	No	10	26	6	8	10	8
	Yes	16	14	7	11	14	4
55—64	No	18	47	10	22	4	13
	Yes	28	21	39	39	14	2
65—69	No	3	13	5	16	0	4
	Yes	11	5	27	16	3	2

mous data of Table 4.10, one parameter per cell describes the dependence relation.

One advantage of the formulation of eqn. (4.18) is that once the maximum likelihood estimates of this equation have been calculated for each cell, reparameterization involves only simple addition and subtraction (as for the estimates of the parameters of eqn. (4.15) in the example of the previous section). This is true for the mathematical model for dependence relationships. From eqn. (4.19), for bivariate dichotomous data the parameter measuring dependence is

$$\psi_{11} = \frac{1}{4}(\log q_{11} - \log q_{12} - \log q_{21} + \log q_{22}) \qquad (4.32)$$

for each cell. The maximum likelihood estimate of ψ_{11} may be calculated from the maximum likelihood estimates of eqn. (4.18) for each cell by addition and subtraction, since the $\dot{q}$ appears in each term and thus cancels, or from eqn. (4.24) directly. The mathematical model is

$$\psi_{ijkl} = \mu_{kl} + \alpha_{ikl} + \beta_{jkl} + \gamma_{ijkl} \qquad (4.33)$$

with the usual constraints.

For the data of Table 4.10, the maximum likelihood estimates, obtained by solving linear equations, are

116

$\hat{\mu} = -0.328$ $\hat{\alpha}_1 = +0.471$ $\hat{\gamma}_{11} = -0.163$ $\hat{\gamma}_{12} = +0.004$ $\hat{\gamma}_{13} = +0.159$
$\hat{\beta}_1 = +0.048$ $\hat{\alpha}_2 = +0.165$ $\hat{\gamma}_{21} = -0.157$ $\hat{\gamma}_{22} = -0.090$ $\hat{\gamma}_{23} = +0.247$
$\hat{\beta}_2 = +0.293$ $\hat{\alpha}_3 = -0.102$ $\hat{\gamma}_{31} = +0.070$ $\hat{\gamma}_{32} = -0.060$ $\hat{\gamma}_{33} = -0.010$
$\hat{\beta}_3 = -0.341$ $\hat{\alpha}_4 = -0.534$ $\hat{\gamma}_{41} = +0.250$ $\hat{\gamma}_{42} = +0.146$ $\hat{\gamma}_{43} = -0.396$

The subscripts k, l have been dropped, since $k=1$, $l=1$ for all values in this dichotomous example. The count n_{4311} has been set arbitrarily at 10^{-2} for illustrative purposes. This value does not greatly distort the estimates. (The model could be constructed with, for example, one less interaction parameter and the estimates obtained by maximizing the likelihood function. As with the example for babies crying in Section 3.4, this zero value does not affect the formulation of likelihood inferences.)

The overall tendency, measured by $\hat{\mu}$, is to a divergence in the responses to the two questions. The values of $\hat{\alpha}_i$ demonstrate that the individuals tend to answer the two questions differently more frequently with increased age. Similarity of response to the two questions also varies greatly among cities.

Mathematical models similar to eqn. (4.33) can also be constructed for the other parameters of probability model (4.19). However, as will be seen below, all of the required parameters are included in the extension of model (4.25) to four variables. But construction of this complete model is not necessary in order to make inferences about a specific model of interest, *i.e.* about eqn. (4.33). For example, the relative likelihood (4.23) may be extended to include the two independent variables by addition of appropriate subscripts to all the parameters. Then, ψ_{ijkl} is replaced by eqn. (4.33), the function is maximized over the parameters λ_{ijk} and ρ_{ijl} and inferences made about the parameters μ_{kl}, α_{ikl}, β_{jkl}, γ_{ijkl}. A second, exactly equivalent alternative with two dichotomous responses is to solve the eqns. (4.32) and (4.33) for one of the original parameters

$$p_{ij11} = \frac{p_{ij12}p_{ij21} \exp[4(\mu_{11} + \alpha_{i11} + \beta_{j11} + y_{ij11})]}{p_{ij22}}$$

and substitute this into the log likelihood function

$$\sum_i \sum_j [4n_{ij11}(\mu_{11} + \alpha_{i11} + \beta_{j11} + y_{ij11}) + n_{ij1.} \log p_{ij12} +$$

$$n_{ij.1} \log p_{ij21} + (n_{ij22} - n_{ij11}) \log p_{ij22}]$$

with only two of the three remaining parameters, p_{ijkl}, independent for each pair (i,j). The relative likelihood function is formed and maximized over the $IJ(K-2)$ remaining parameters, p_{ijkl}, and inferences are made about the parameters of interest.

With a multivariate response, independence relationships become more complex. With a bivariate response variable (j,k) and one independent variable (i), the situation in between models (4.15) and (4.25), eqn. (4.19) becomes

$$\log(p_{ijk}/\dot{p}_i) = \lambda_{ij} + \rho_{ik} + \psi_{ijk} \tag{4.34}$$

Here, parameters with the same subscripts are not identical to those of models (4.15) and (4.25). Instead, $\lambda_{ij} = \rho_j + \psi_{ij}$, $\rho_{ik} = \kappa_k + \eta_{ik}$, and $\psi_{ijk} = \xi_{jk} + \tau_{ijk}$ of model (4.25) or the equivalent from model (4.15). If $\psi_{ijk} = 0$ (all i,j,k), the two response variables are marginally independent conditional on the value of the independent variable

$$p_{ijk} = p_{i.k}p_{ij.} \quad \text{or} \quad q_{ijk} = q_{i.k}q_{ij.}/q_{i..} \tag{4.35}$$

which is the same as eqn. (4.29). For this structure, the mathematical model (4.31) becomes

$$\log(p_{ijk}/\dot{p}_i) = \mu_{jk} + \alpha_{ijk} \tag{4.36}$$

with

$$\sum_j\sum_k \mu_{jk} = 0, \quad \sum_i \alpha_{ijk} = \sum_j\sum_k \alpha_{ijk} = 0$$

Here, $\mu_{jk} = \rho_j + \kappa_k + \xi_{jk}$ and $\alpha_{ijk} = \psi_{ij} + \eta_{ik} + \tau_{ijk}$ in model (4.25) or the equivalent in model (4.15). This model (4.36) might equivalently be constructed individually for each of the parameters of probability model (4.34), as was done in the example, yielding a model similar to (4.25) but with λ_i missing. If $\alpha_{ijk} = 0$ (all i,j,k) in eqn. (4.36)

$$p_{ijk} = p_{jk} \quad \text{or} \quad q_{ijk} = q_{i..}q_{.jk}/q_{...} \tag{4.37}$$

which is the same as eqns. (4.27) and (4.28), but with a different pair of variables jointly independent of the third. Many other types of independence may also be constructed, as other response and independent variables are added.

In normal theory analysis of data, the measure of (linear)

118

association, the correlation coefficient, and of conditional dependence, the linear regression coefficient, are distinct (although if one is zero so is the other). The analogous (in this case, non-linear) measures for the multinomial distribution are identical. The same parameter values and inferences are obtained whether X_1 is assumed to be distributed conditionally on (4.15) or jointly with (4.25) X_2 and X_3. This useful feature arises from the way in which the log function is normalized in eqns. (4.14) and (4.18). Consider, for example, the situation of eqns. (4.34) and (4.36).

$$\log(p_{ijk}/\dot{p}_i) = \log p_{ijk} - \frac{1}{JK} \sum_j \sum_k \log p_{ijk}$$

$$= \log(q_{ijk}/q_{i..}) - \frac{1}{JK} \sum_j \sum_k \log(q_{ijk}/q_{i..})$$

$$= \log q_{ijk} - \frac{1}{JK} \sum_j \sum_k \log q_{ijk} = \log(q_{ijk}/\dot{q}_i)$$

In the same way, $\log(p_{ijk}/\dot{p}) = \log(q_{ijk}/\dot{q})$ in eqn. (4.25), etc. When normalized by their geometric means, joint (q) and conditional (p) probabilities are identical if the same number of variables are present. The parameters appearing in a model will depend on which geometric mean is used, as in eqns. (4.15), (4.25), (4.34), and (4.36), but those parameters present in two models *containing the same number of variables* will be identical or linear sums. These equations may be solved for the parameters of the model. For example, from eqn. (4.25), $\xi_{jk} = \log(\dot{q}_{jk}\dot{q}/\dot{q}_j\dot{q}_k)$ and $\tau_{ijk} = \log(q_{ijk}\dot{q}_i\dot{q}_j\dot{q}_k/\dot{q}_{ij}\dot{q}_{ik}\dot{q}_{jk}\dot{q})$, and the same for β_{jk} and γ_{ijk} from eqn. (4.15) (with p replacing q). From eqn. (4.34), $\psi_{ijk} = \log(p_{ijk}\dot{p}_i/\dot{p}_{ij}\dot{p}_{ik}) = \xi_{jk} + \tau_{ijk} = \beta_{jk} + \gamma_{ijk}$, etc.

Suppose now that the sociologist is analyzing the dependence chain of eqn. (3.26)

$$P(X_1,X_2,X_3) = P(X_1/X_2,X_3)P(X_2/X_3)P(X_3)$$

For $P(X_1/X_2,X_3)$, model (4.15) is applied, or the appropriate parameters (κ_k, η_{ik}, ξ_{jk}, τ_{ijk}) chosen from model (4.25). For $P(X_2/X_3)$, model (4.19) (replacing subscript k by j), or equivalently the polychotomous extension of model (3.7), is used. But, model (4.25) also contains parameters (ψ_{ij}) describing a relationship between X_2 and X_3. Why are these not used instead? In a recursive system such as that given above, a time sequence in the appearance of the variables is usually assumed to apply: X_3, X_2, X_1. Then, the distribution of X_2 depends on the value of X_3 before X_1 has occurred. But, the parameters ψ_{ij} in model (4.25) give the relationship between X_2 and X_3 with the effects of X_1 removed (as with a partial correlation coefficient). Since X_1 is assumed not yet to have occurred, model (4.19) is appropriate. If $P(X_2/X_3)P(X_3)$ is replaced by $P(X_2,X_3)$ in the model, *i.e.* if X_2 and X_3 precede X_1 in time with no order between X_2 and X_3, the analysis is the same as above since model (4.19) for $P(X_2,X_3)$ is identical to the extension of model (3.7) for $P(X_2/X_3)$. A third possibility, $P(X_1,X_2/X_3)$, uses models (4.34) and (4.36), which have been seen to be derivable from model (4.25). The fourth situation arises if a time sequence is not discernible at all. The parameters of eqn. (4.25) are all used to analyze the joint distribution, $P(X_1,X_2,X_3)$, without factoring it into conditional distributions. This gives association or reciprocal dependence among all of the variables, and *cannot* be interpreted, for example, as the dependence of the distribution of each variable in turn on the values of the other two, *i.e.* consecutive application of model (4.15) changing subscripts (dependent variable). Goodman (1972) uses this last model (4.25) in his analysis, thus looking at association and not at conditionality or causality.

The set of statistical models chosen to describe the phenomena under study will depend on the (time) structure of the data. Although the estimated parameter values and the maximum relative likelihoods for some of the relationships will be identical for two different structures, their interpretation (association or conditional dependence) will depend on the structure among the other variables.

4.5 Inferences for Models with Many Parameters

Many of the models discussed, especially in this chapter, contain a very large number of parameters. Exact inferences must be made by considering a likelihood function which describes a multidimensional surface. In order to conceptualize this surface, maximization of the function over all parameters except one or two has been used. In this way, a profile or silhouette of the multidimensional surface is obtained. But the maximum relative likelihood graphs will often tend to be wider than necessary, providing less precise inferences about the parameters than might otherwise be available.

One way of surmounting this problem occurs automatically if the likelihood function factors into several parts, each containing different parameters. In this case, when inferences are made about the parameters in one part using a ratio of likelihoods, all of the parameters in the other parts disappear through cancellation. Fortunately, for the logistic type models (those analogous to analysis of variance, but not the regression models) used throughout this book, the likelihood function usually is very close to factorization into parts containing the different types of parameters in the model, e.g. with the two variable interaction models (3.15) and (4.15), into four parts containing the sets of parameters μ, α_i, β_j, and γ_{ij} respectively. Thus, maximization of the relative likelihood function leads to very little loss of precision. This result was used to obtain the approximate relative likelihoods of Section 4.2.

For a special group of statistical models, which includes all of the logistic models of this book, a more exact technique may be applied. Suppose that the parameters are divided into those of interest and a remaining set of nuisance parameters. If all of the information in the data about the nuisance parameters may be summarized in a limited number of measures derived from the data (called sufficient statistics), the conditional probability distribution (see Section 3.3) of the data, given these statistics, will not contain the nuisance parameters. A conditional likelihood function is derived from this distribution in the same way as the ordinary function from the ordinary distribution. For the logistic models, the maximum likelihood estimates (or any one-to-one function of them) are the required sufficient statistics.

Derivations of such conditional probability distributions are usually complex and will not be discussed here; Cox (1970, Chap. 4) and Kalbfleisch and Sprott (1970) provide details. Rasch (1960, 1961) gives an excellent discussion of how this method is relevant to some social science problems. As an example of the effect of this procedure, the questionnaire data of Table 3.6, discussed in Section 3.4, may be reconsidered. The statistical model with interaction (3.15) contains eight parameters. Since the effect of differences in experience (β_1) is of interest, the maximum relative likelihood graph for this parameter, as plotted in Fig. 3.4, is reproduced in Fig. 4.1. For comparison, the conditional relative likelihood function has also been plotted in the same figure. With seven parameters eliminated, this graph is slight-

121

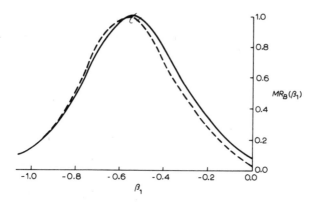

Fig. 4.1 The maximum relative likelihood graph (solid curve) reproduced from Fig. 3.4, maximized over the seven remaining parameters of mathematical model (3.15) and the corresponding conditional relative likelihood graph (broken line) which eliminates the seven parameters by using the conditional distribution, showing the slightly increased precision of inferences when maximization is not required.

ly narrower, yielding more precise inferences, but the difference is comparable to that obtained using the no-interaction model (3.18), also illustrated in Fig. 3.4.

Adequate description of this conditional procedure is beyond the scope of this book; the reader is referred to the references cited above. But, as with the use of all conditional distributions, the need for extreme care must be emphasized. If one parameter is chosen for inference making using the conditional argument, this parameter cannot later be considered as a nuisance parameter and conditioned out, since contradictions in the inferences will result. The inferences about the parameters must be placed in some logical order and a series of conditional distributions derived as in eqn. (3.27) in the same way as is required for deriving the complex dependence relationships of Section 3.5.

CHAPTER 5

Data Reduction and Classification

5.1 Comparison and Grouping of Individuals

Often, a large number of characteristics is recorded for each of a group of individuals. The sociologist wishes to be able to form sub-groups of individuals according to how similar the characteristics are for each individual. This problem can take a number of forms. One of the variables, a response, may be of principal interest and the sociologist wishes to split the sample into homogeneous groups according to the other characteristics recorded, with the various groups having a maximum difference in the distribution of this response variable. This procedure, called the method of segmentation, is discussed in Section 5.4. One example is the analysis of the percentage of people voting for a party, dividing the sample by the use of such independent variables as age, sex, social class, salary, region of the country, etc.

If the characteristics recorded are not split into one response and a number of independent variables, the problem is often the reverse. The sociologist wishes to group the individuals according to similarity as to the characteristics measured. Instead of splitting the sample into smaller and smaller groups according to the segmentation procedure, the individuals are grouped into successively larger groups until the complete sample is reached. In section 5.3, a method of performing this classification is described. If a group of individuals is asked a number of different questions, the sociologist may want to group the individuals according to the similarity of their responses to the questions.

A third problem of this type was discussed briefly in Section 2.3. A response variable takes a large number of values and the sociologist wishes to group the responses according to similarity of various independent variables observed. If the dependent variable is occupation, the sociologist may group these into larger social categories using the observed values of a number of independent variables such as salary, membership in clubs, education, etc. This problem may be considered as a composite of the previous two. The sample is first split into groups according to the values of the dependent variable observed, as in segmentation. Then, these groups are combined according to the similarity of the observed values of the independent variables, as in classification.

In all of these analyses, an initial problem often appears. A very large number of variables has been recorded for each individual. Only a few will be of prime importance in performing the analysis, the others either providing little information or redundant information about the groups to be produced. In order to reduce the amount of calculation in obtaining the groups, the number of variables should be reduced to the several important ones. The method of reduction will depend on the type of grouping problem to be performed afterwards.

An important paper in the field of data reduction for survey analysis is that of Sonquist and Morgan (1963).

5.2 Reducing the Number of Variables

Suppose that a large number of variables is recorded for the individuals in a sample with the intent to group the individuals according to their similarity as measured by the variables recorded. This set of variables, X_1, X_2, X_3, X_4,... has a multivariate multinomial distribution as used in Sections 3.3 and 4.4, where $q_{ijkl...}$ is the proportion of individuals in the overall population having values x_{1i}, x_{2j}, x_{3k}, x_{4l},... of the variables, and $n_{ijkl...}$ the number in the sample having these observed values. (The dots represent other subscripts and not summation as in previous chapters.)

If one of the variables may very plausibly be distributed marginally independently of the others, this implies that it carries information about the individuals which is very different from that of the other variables. Conversely, if independence is implausible, the information provided by this variable is already available through the other variables. Thus, variables with implausible independence may be eliminated. If the variable X_1 is independent of the remaining variables, the multivariate probability distribution, given here for only four variables to simplify notation, decomposes

$$P(X_1,X_2,X_3,X_4) = P(X_1)P(X_2,X_3,X_4) \qquad (5.1)$$

the extension of eqn. (4.27). In order for the multivariate multinomial distribution to decompose in this way, the probabilities must have the form $q_{ijkl} = q_{i...}q_{.jkl}$. With maximum likelihood estimates $\hat{q}_{ijkl} = n_{ijkl}/n_{....}$, the log relative likelihood function is

$$\log R_M(q_{ijkl}) = \sum_i \sum_j \sum_k \sum_l n_{ijkl}(\log q_{ijkl} - \log \hat{q}_{ijkl}) \qquad (5.2)$$

Since $n_{i...}$ (dots signifying summation in this discussion with four variables) is the number of times that x_{1i} is observed in the sample, the maximum likelihood estimates are $\hat{q}_{i...} = n_{i...}/n_{....}$ and $\hat{q}_{.jkl} = n_{.jkl}/n_{....}$. The plausibility of X_1 being marginally independent of X_2, X_3, X_4 is given by

$$\log R_M(q_{ijkl} = \hat{q}_{i...}\hat{q}_{.jkl}) = \sum_i \sum_j \sum_k \sum_l n_{ijkl} \log \left[\frac{n_{i...}\,n_{.jkl}}{n_{....}\,n_{ijkl}} \right] \qquad (5.3)$$

This relative likelihood is calculated for each variable in turn, and the variable with the smallest value of R_M (most negative value of $\log R_M$) eliminated. The process is then repeated with the remaining variables, continuing until some criterion is met. The criterion may be that a minimum number of variables (say 4 or 5) must remain, or that all of the relative likelihoods be greater than a certain value.

At first sight, it might appear that one could stop at the first stage after calculating the value of eqn. (5.3) for each variable and then eliminate immediately all those with small plausibilities until one of the criteria given above is met. But suppose that, say, X_3 and X_5 each have small plausibilities of independence from all the other variables so that they are eliminated simultaneously. This small plausibility may be due to a high degree of dependence between X_3 and X_5 with virtual independence from all other variables. Both will be eliminated, and the information they contain lost, whereas one should be retained. This invalidates any simultaneous elimination.

If one of the observed variables is to be used as a response variable, the preceding procedure is not valid, since the conditional distribution is used in making inferences. In this case, the extension of eqns. (4.6) and (4.8) to many independent variables may

125

be used. If the distribution of the response Y does not change as X_1 takes different values, the relationship

$$P(Y/X_1, X_2, X_3, ...) = P(Y/X_2, X_3, ...) \qquad (5.4)$$

holds, as the extension of eqn. (4.29). For the observed values, x_{1i}, x_{2j}, x_{3l}, ..., the probability of the response being $y_{ijl...k}$ is $p_{ijl...k}$, with maximum likelihood estimate

$$\hat{p}_{ijl...k} = n_{ijl...k} \Big/ \sum_k n_{ijl...k}$$

(For the rest of this section, dots indicate other indices and not summation.) If the distribution of the response Y does not depend on the value of X_1 observed, $p_{ijl...k} = p_{jl...k}$ no matter what value, x_{1i}, is observed. The maximum likelihood estimate is

$$\hat{p}_{jl...k} = \sum_i n_{ijl...k} \Big/ \sum_i \sum_k n_{ijl...k}$$

With log relative likelihood function

$$\log R_M(p_{ijl...k}) = \sum_i \sum_j \sum_l ... \sum_k n_{ijl...k} (\log p_{ijl...k} - \log \hat{p}_{ijl...k})$$

$$(5.5)$$

the measure of plausibility of the distribution of Y being conditionally independent of X_1 given all of the other variables is

$$\log R_M(p_{ijl...k} = \hat{p}_{jl...k}) =$$

$$\sum_i \sum_j \sum_l ... \sum_k n_{ijl...k} \log \left[\frac{(\sum_i n_{ijl...k})(\sum_k n_{ijl...k})}{(n_{ijl...k})(\sum_i \sum_k n_{ijl...k})} \right] \qquad (5.6)$$

After this relative likelihood has been calculated for each independent variable, the variable from which the distribution of Y is most plausibly independent is eliminated. As with eqn. (4.29), both the main effect and all interactions containing the variable must be implausible. Note that in this case, the variable having the largest value of eqn. (5.6) (the value of $\log R_M$ closest to zero) is eliminated, whereas in the previous procedure, the variable with the smallest value of eqn. (5.3) (most negative value of $\log R_M$) was eliminated.

The value of eqn. (5.6) is recalculated for each of the remaining

126

variables and a second one eliminated. Again, a criterion is established and the process repeated until it is met. In certain cases when little is known about a study before a sample is taken so that a large number of variables are recorded, this second procedure may be applied before going on to use the methods of Chapters 3 and 4.

5.3 Classification

A number of polychotomous variables have been observed for a sample of individuals. The sociologist wishes to group the individuals according to similarity as measured by the observed values of the variables. If a large number of variables has been recorded, the number may be reduced by the first procedure of Section 5.2.

In the first stage of grouping, the individuals are compared in pairs to determine the plausibility that the members of each pair have similar values of the variables. The pair with the greatest plausibility is combined. The process is repeated in the next stage considering the combined pair as an individual with two values of each variable. At each stage, one less individual or group will remain until all of the individuals belong to the same group. The division into groups sought may be determined either by the level of plausibility or by the number of groups desired, as illustrated in Fig. 5.1.

Consider the plausibility that the observed values of the variables for two individuals are the same. From eqn. (5.2), the

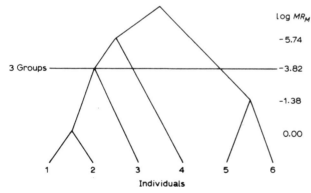

Fig. 5.1 An example of the diagram for classification of six individuals (from Table 5.1) into groups using likelihood methods.

127

maximized log likelihood is

$$\log L_M(\hat{q}_{ijkl...}) = \sum_i \sum_j \sum_k \sum_l ... \ n_{ijkl...} \ (\log \hat{q}_{ijkl...}) \qquad (5.7)$$

for each individual. But, $n_{ijkl...}$ is 0 or 1 for all values of the subscripts, as is $\hat{q}_{ijkl...}$, so that $\log L_M = 0$ (0 log 0 = 0). When the observed values of the variables are combined for the two individuals, $n_{ijkl...}$ will again be 0 or 1 for all values of the subscripts unless the two individuals have the same values for all the variables. Then, $\log L_M = 2 \log 0.5$ unless the two individuals have the same values for all variables, as does the log relative likelihood. Thus, this procedure only groups those individuals giving exactly the same response to all variables and is of extremely limited value.

In order to derive a useful method, some additional assumption must be made. Suppose that all of the observed variables may plausibly be considered to be distributed with complete marginal independence, eqn. (4.26), usually only after application of the procedure of Section 5.2. Then, $q_{1i}, q_{2j}, q_{3k}, q_{4l}, ...$ are the probabilities of observing respectively the values $x_{1i}, x_{2j}, x_{3k}, x_{4l}, ...$ of the variables $X_1, X_2, X_3, X_4, ...$ and $q_{ijkl...} = q_{1i}q_{2j}q_{3k}q_{4l}...$. The maximized log likelihood is

$$\log L_M(\hat{q}_{1i}, \hat{q}_{2j}, \hat{q}_{3k}, \hat{q}_{4l}, ...) = \sum_i n_{1i} \log \hat{q}_{1i} + \sum_j n_{2j} \log \hat{q}_{2j} + ...$$
$$(5.8)$$

Again, $n_{1i}, n_{2j}, n_{3k}, n_{4l}, ...$ will be 0 or 1 for all values of the subscripts, for each individual, as will $\hat{q}_{1i}, \hat{q}_{2j}, \hat{q}_{3k}, \hat{q}_{4l}, ...$ so that $\log L_M = 0$. But, when the observed values are combined for two individuals, $n_{1i} = 2$ if both individuals have x_{1i}, $n_{1i} = 1$ if one individual has x_{1i}, and $n_{1i} = 0$ otherwise. Then, either $n_{1i} = 0$ for all except one value of i, for which $n_{1i} = 2$ or $n_{1i} = 0$ for all except two values of i, for which $n_{1i} = 1$. The same holds for $n_{2j}, n_{3k}, n_{4l}, ...$. Consider now the values of $\hat{q}_{1i}$. If $n_{1i} = 2$ for a value of i, $\hat{q}_{1i} = 1$ for that value of i and zero for all others. If $n_{1i} = 1$ for two values of i, $\hat{q}_{1i} = 0.5$ for those two values of i and zero otherwise. Again, this is applied to $q_{2j}, q_{3k}, q_{4l}, ...$. If $\hat{q}_{1i} = 1$, i.e. if both individuals have the same value of X_1, the corresponding term, $\Sigma n_{1i} \log \hat{q}_{1i}$ of eqn. (5.8) will be zero in the combined likelihood for the two individuals. If $\hat{q}_{1i} = 0.5$ for two values of i and zero otherwise, i.e. if the two individuals have different values of X_1, the term $\Sigma n_{1i} \log \hat{q}_{1i}$ will be 2 log 0.5. The total log likelihood is $2a_2 \log 0.5$ where a_2 is the number of variables for which the two individuals give different responses. Since the log likelihood for each individual separately is zero, the log relative likelihood of a pair of individuals having the same response on all variables is

$$R_M(2 \text{ individuals similar}) = 2a_2 \log 0.5 \qquad (5.9)$$

Note that this is a negative number. This comparison is made for all pairs of individuals and the pair with the value of eqn. (5.9) largest (closest to zero), $i.e.$ the pair with the smallest number a_2 of differences in response, is combined.

The procedure is repeated considering this pair combined. All of the calculations from the previous stage may be reused, but the plausibility of combining each remaining individual with the pair must be obtained. The total log likelihood for the pair and the individual to be different is $0 + 2a_2 \log 0.5$. That for the three to be combined must be calculated. If all three individuals give the same response to X_1, $n_{1i} = 3$ and $\hat{q}_{1i} = 1$ for some value of i and zero for all others. If two give the same response and one different, $n_{1i} = 1$ and 2 and $\hat{q}_{1i} = 1/3$ and 2/3 for two values of i, and zero otherwise. If all three responses are different, $n_{1i} = 1$ and $\hat{q}_{1i} = 1/3$ for three values of i and zero otherwise. (This procedure is, of course, limited by the number of possible values of X_1). The term $\Sigma n_{1i} \log \hat{q}_{1i}$ in eqn. (5.8) is zero if all 3 individuals give the same response, $\log 1/3 + 2 \log 2/3$ if 2 individuals give the same response to X_1, and $3 \log 1/3$ if all 3 responses are different. The sum of the terms for all variables gives the log likelihood of combining the individual with the pair

$$\log L_M = a_3 (\log 1/3 + 2 \log 2/3) + b_3 (3 \log 1/3)$$

where a_3 is the number of variables for which 2 individuals of the 3 are in agreement and b_3 the number for which all 3 are in disagreement. The log relative likelihood of combining an individual with a pair is

$$\log R_M(3 \text{ individuals similar}) = (a_3 + 3b_3) \log 1/3 + 2a_3 \log 2/3$$

$$- 2a_2 \log 0.5 \qquad (5.10)$$

At this stage, two types of plausibilities must be compared: those for combining two of the remaining individuals into a second pair and those of combining an individual with the first pair to form a triplet. The combination with the largest plausibility is performed, yielding either a triplet and the rest individuals or two pairs and the rest individuals. If a triplet has been formed, plausibilities of combining an individual with a triplet must be calculated. The resulting log likelihood is

$$\log L_M = a_4 (\log 1/4 + 3 \log 3/4) + b_4 (2 \log 2/4 + 2 \log 2/4)$$

$$+ c_4 (2 \log 2/4 + 2 \log 1/4) + d_4 (4 \log 1/4)$$

where a_4 is the number of variables for which 3 individuals are in agreement, b_4 2 individuals choose each of 2 responses, c_4 2 individuals are in agreement and 2 in disagreement, and d_4 all 4 individuals are in disagreement. The log relative likelihood is

$$\log R_M (1 \text{ individual similar to triplet}) = (a_4 + 2c_4 + 4d_4) \log 1/4$$

$$+ (4b_4 + 2c_4) \log 0.5 + 3a_4 \log 3/4 - (a_3 + 3b_3) \log 1/3$$

$$- 2a_3 \log 2/3 \tag{5.11}$$

If, at the second stage, a second pair was formed instead of a triplet, at the third stage, plausibility of combining the two pairs must be calculated, as measured by the log relative likelihood

$$\log R_M (2 \text{ pairs similar}) = (a_4 + 2c_4 + 4d_4) \log 1/4$$

$$+ (4b_4 + 2c_4) \log 0.5 + 3a_4 \log 3/4 - 2(a_2 + a_2') \log 0.5 \tag{5.12}$$

Note that although both eqns. (5.11) and (5.12) give the plausibility of grouping 4 individuals, they differ because of the different combinations previously formed.

Many other possibilities are to be found as the process of combination continues. In general, the log relative likelihood of combining two groups, whether each group contains one or more individuals, is calculated from eqn. (5.8) as

$$\log R_{M12} = \log L_{M12} - \log L_{M1} - \log L_{M2} \tag{5.13}$$

where $\log L_{M1}$ and $\log L_{M2}$ are obtained by calculating eqn. (5.8) separately for each of the two groups and $\log L_{M12}$ after combining the groups. At each stage, eqn. (5.13) is calculated for each possible pair of groups (with one or more individuals in a group), the largest value selected, and that pair of groups combined. Note that from stage to stage, eqn. (5.13) will remain the same for most pairs of comparisons made and need only be recalculated if one member of the pair is combined with some other group.

With this procedure, a missing value of a response to one of the variables by an individual may automatically be treated as a

TABLE 5.1

Yes/no responses of six individuals to seven questions with two responses missing.

Question	Individual					
	1	2	3	4	5	6
1	Y	Y	Y	N	N	N
2	Y	Y	Y	Y	N	N
3	Y	Y		N	N	Y
4	N	N	N	N	N	N
5	N	N	N	N	Y	Y
6	N	N	N	N	Y	Y
7	N	N	Y		Y	Y

further possible observed value of the variable. If, say, X_3 has K possible values and is missing for an individual, this is treated as a $(K+1)$th value of X_3.

The application of this procedure does not necessarily require continuation until all individuals have been combined into one group unless a complete diagram, such as Fig. 5.1 is to be constructed. Otherwise, the process may be stopped after the plausibility of any further combination of groups is sufficiently small or after the desired number of groups has been obtained.

Consider the responses of six individuals to seven yes/no questions with two missing values given in Table 5.1. The log relative likelihood of combining individuals 1 and 2 is zero so that these form the first group. With $\log R_M = -1.38$, individuals 5 and 6 are combined at the second stage. At the next stage, the combination (3,4) has $\log R_M = -4.16$, the combination (1,2,3), $\log R_M = -3.82$, and (4,5,6), $\log R_M = -8.17$ so that the second is chosen giving groups (1,2,3), (4), and (5,6). In the final stage, the combination (1,2,3,4) has $\log R_M = -5.74$ and (4,5,6) has $\log R_M = -8.17$. The resulting diagram was given in Fig. 5.1. All of the possible comparisons have not been given at each stage in this simple example, since some combinations may be eliminated by inspection. In general, all possible combinations should be calculated, especially after the first stage.

5.4 Segmentation

Suppose that some polychotomous response, together with

131

several independent variables, is measured on a large number of individuals. The sociologist wishes to split the sample into a number of smaller groups so that the distribution of the response variable has maximum difference among groups. If a large number of different independent variables has been recorded, the number may be reduced by the second procedure of Section 5.2.

The procedure of Section 4.2 is applied in turn to determine the dependence of the distribution of the response variable on each separate independent variable, using the relative likelihood (4.2). The independent variable giving the smallest value of the relative likelihood is chosen, *i.e.* that variable from which the distribution of the response is least plausibly independent, and the sample is split into groups according to the observed values of this independent variable.

At the second stage, the same procedure is repeated within each group using the remaining independent variables. The independent variable chosen at this and succeeding stages may differ among groups. Each group produced at the first stage is subdivided into further groups according to the observed value of the independent variable chosen for that group. At each stage, all independent variables which have not previously been used in forming that particular group are considered. Figure 5.2 gives a representative diagram for the first two stages of the segmentation of the votes for three parties in an election.

The number of divisions of a group at any stage depends on the number of different observed values of that variable which has been found to give the most difference in response distribution.

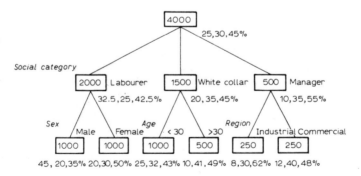

Fig. 5.2 A fictitious example of the first two steps of the segmentation by likelihood methods of the voters in an election according to the observed values of various independent variables.

Often, several values of the independent variable will produce little difference in the response distribution within the group, *i.e.* will have high plausibility of identical effect as discussed in Section 4.2 for eqn. (4.2). These values may be combined, yielding fewer divisions of the group. The same procedure may be used if the sociologist only wishes to split a group into, say, two parts at each stage. In Fig. 5.2, at the first stage, white collar workers and managers might be combined. On the other hand, the age division has obviously already been grouped in the analysis. If the response measured is dichotomous, the procedures of Section 4.2 reduce to those of Section 3.2.

Since this analysis involves a straightforward application of procedures previously discussed in detail, a more complete numerical example will not be given.

5.5 Reducing the Number of Values of the Response Variable

In this section, the reduction problem of Chapter 2 will be reconsidered for the case when additional information about similarity in the observed values of a polychotomous response variable is available in the form of the corresponding values of a number of independent variables. The values of a response variable are recorded for a large number of individuals, with the variable taking a large number of different values. The sociologist wishes to group these values or outcomes into a smaller number of labels using the available information provided by a number of independent variables. If too many independent variables are available, some may be eliminated by the second procedure of Section 5.2.

The individuals are naturally divided into a number of groups according to the observed values of the response variable (segmented, but using the dependent instead of the independent variable). The classification procedure of Section 5.3 is applied to these groups using eqn. (5.13) and the available independent variables. Thus, this procedure begins with the individuals already partially grouped or classified, according to the observed values of the response variable. From another point of view, the observed outcomes, labels, or response variable values are classified as to similarity using the information provided by the independent variables.

Since the procedure of Section 5.3 is applied directly, this application does not require further discussion.

CHAPTER 6

A Specialized Example:
Social Mobility

6.1 Analysis of Social Mobility

Some of the more sophisticated examples of the application of statistical analysis to sociological data occur in the field of social mobility. This is probably due to the ideological interest of western countries in this aspect of society. The problem may be considered at two levels. Change in social status may be analyzed between generations in which case only limited data are usually available (between two generations). Or, mobility may be analyzed within a generation, *e.g.* within a lifetime or within a factory. Here, a series of observations may be available at different points in time.

The literature on social mobility is very extensive (see, for example, Boudon, 1973); no attempt will be made here to provide an exhaustive treatment. Several simple examples will be given to illustrate the approach using likelihood inferences. Attention will be restricted to intergenerational mobility although the same models may also be applied to the intragenerational case.

Two separate approaches have been made to the problem of social mobility. Originally, sociologists sought a measure or index of mobility in a society. As will be seen in Section 6.2, construction of such an index involves the condensation of a large amount of data into a single number. Not only is much information lost, but also the interpretation of the index will depend on how the condensation is performed.

134

In the second approach, the sociologist attempts to describe and explain the process of social mobility. In simple models, such as those discussed in Section 6.3, only the social mobility data themselves are analyzed to determine their structure. Recently, more complex models have been constructed (Boudon reviews these and suggests several others) involving the introduction of external independent variables such as fertility, education, etc. In spite of these complications, they require few special statistical procedures not discussed in this book, and hence will not be considered separately.

6.2 Indices of Social Mobility

In its simplest form, information on social mobility between generations is summarized in a table such as Table 3.2, giving the social statuses of fathers and sons with only two possible categories (a first method of condensation of the information). Mobility is a measure of how many sons have changed from their fathers' social category. Indeed, the measure of dependence given by eqn. (3.3) for such a table is a valid measure of mobility (or, as will be seen below, immobility): if $\alpha_1 = 0$, the son's category does not depend on the father's and the mobility is perfect; if $\alpha_1 = -\infty$, the maximum number of sons have changed from the category of their father; if $\alpha_1 = +\infty$, the son's category is completely dependent on the father's. (Using the transformed values of α_1 from eqn. (3.8), these become $\alpha_1' = 0$: maximum mobility, $\alpha_1' = 0.5$: perfect mobility, $\alpha_1' = 1$: minimum mobility.) For Table 3.2, the mobility with $\hat{\alpha}_1 = 0.46$ ($\hat{\alpha}_1' = 0.61$) is slightly less than perfect (*i.e.* towards minimum mobility), but as was seen in Section 3.2, the data provide no evidence that the mobility is not perfect (*i.e.* $\alpha_1 = 0.0$ or $\alpha_1' = 0.5$ is very plausible, as shown in Fig. 3.2).

An advantage of the index of eqn. (3.3) is that inferences may easily be made about the mobility in a sample when more than two social categories are present. In this case, the polychotomous extension of eqn. (3.7) has $(K-1)^2$ independent parameters α_{ik} and the procedures of Sections 4.2 and 4.3 are used. For example, eqn. (4.2) gives the plausibility of perfect mobility when any number of social classes are present. If $R_M(p_{ik} = \hat{p}_k) = 1.0$, the observed mobility is perfect and as R_M approaches zero, the hypothesis of perfect mobility decreases in plausibility. Since maximum and minimum mobility are not as clearly defined for more than two social categories, and since mobility greater than perfect should occur only exceptionally, the value of R_M will often be sufficient indication of mobility. The larger the value of R_M, between zero and one, the greater the plausible mobility. If the value of R_M calculated for a table is small, the assumption that mobility is close to the minimum and not to the maximum may be verified by inspection. If the diagonal elements (n_{ik} with $i=k$) tend to be large as compared to off-diagonal elements, the mobility is minimum and conversely. This also applies to only two social categories: for Table 3.2, $MR_B(\alpha_1=0) = 0.70$ showing again that plausibility of perfect mobility is very high.

The difference in interpretation of α_1 and of $MR_B(\alpha_1=0)$ (or of $R_M(p_{ik}=\hat{p}_k)$) must be kept in mind. The index α_1 measures the distance from perfect (in the direction of maximum or minimum) mobility, but gives no indication of how plausible is the value obtained. Conversely, the relative likelihood provides only the plausibility and no measure of distance. But, with more than two social categories, no single unique index is available. As was seen in Section 3.2, the relative likelihood depends on the size of the sample. Table 3.3 gives $MR_B(\alpha_1=0) = 0.02$ while the measure of social mobility $\hat{\alpha}_1 = 0.46$ remains the same as in Table 3.2. The value $\hat{\alpha}_1$ has little meaning unless a measure of plausibility is available, such as illustrated in Fig. 3.2 or at least the value of $MR_B(\alpha_1=0)$.

A second advantage of using α_1 and $MR_B(\alpha_1=0)$ is contained in the concept of sufficiency, one of the original reasons for adopting the mathematical model (3.2). An index of this form uses all of the information in the data about the mobility. A disadvantage of the index, either in the form of eqn. (3.3) or of eqn. (3.8), is that a direct sociological interpretation is not immediately apparent.

A number of sociologically appealing indices has been developed, usually only for the case of two social categories. Only one will be discussed here, as developed by Boudon (1973) for two social categories, with possible extensions to more than two categories.

Boudon's index is based on the joint distribution of the fathers' and sons' categories, as illustrated in Table 3.4, instead of on the conditional distribution of the son's category given the father's. But, the observed social structure, as determined by the marginal totals of the table of observed data, is considered fixed. The index is defined as the ratio of the observed pure mobility to the total possible pure mobility given the social structure (marginals).

$$\hat{\theta} = \frac{\min(n_{12}, n_{21})}{\min(n_{11}, n_{22}) + \min(n_{12}, n_{21})} \tag{6.1}$$

This is derived as follows: the total mobility observed is $N - \Sigma n_{ii}$ (where $N = n_{..}$), the minimum or structural mobility is $N - \Sigma \min(n_{i.}, n_{.i})$, and the maximum possible mobility as $N - \Sigma'_{i} (n_{i.} - \sum_{j \neq i} n_{.j})$ where Σ' is over non-negative values only. Pure mobility is the difference between observed or maximum and structural so that

$$\hat{\theta} = \frac{(N - \sum_i n_{ii}) - [N - \sum_i \min(n_{i.}, n_{.i})]}{[N - \sum_i' (n_{i.} - \sum_{j \neq i} n_{.j})] - [N - \sum_i \min(n_{i.}, n_{.i})]} \tag{6.2}$$

which reduces to eqn. (6.1) when only two social categories are present.

The relative likelihood function as derived from eqn. (3.10) is

$$R_M(q_{ij}) = \prod_i \prod_j \left[\frac{q_{ij}}{\hat{q}_{ij}}\right]^{n_{ij}} \tag{6.3}$$

In terms of the original parameters, eqn. (6.1) takes four forms according to the data observed.

$$\theta = \frac{q_{12}}{q_{11} + q_{12}} \qquad (n_{12} < n_{21}, n_{11} < n_{22}) \tag{6.4a}$$

$$= \frac{q_{12}}{q_{12} + q_{22}} \qquad (n_{12} < n_{21}, n_{11} > n_{22}) \tag{6.4b}$$

$$= \frac{q_{21}}{q_{11} + q_{21}} \qquad (n_{12} > n_{21}, n_{11} < n_{22}) \tag{6.4c}$$

$$= \frac{q_{21}}{q_{21} + q_{22}} \qquad (n_{12} > n_{21}, n_{11} > n_{22}) \tag{6.4d}$$

Equations (6.4) may be substituted into the relative likelihood equation, eliminating one of the original parameters, either q_{12} or q_{21}.

$$R_M(\theta, q_{11}, q_{22}) = \left[\frac{Nq_{11}}{n_{11}}\right]^{n_{11}} \left[\frac{\theta N q_{11}}{(1-\theta)n_{12}}\right]^{n_{12}} \left[\frac{Nq_{21}}{n_{21}}\right]^{n_{21}}$$

$$\times \left[\frac{Nq_{22}}{n_{22}}\right]^{n_{22}} \tag{6.5a}$$

$$(n_{12} < n_{21}, \; n_{11} < n_{22})$$

$$= \left[\frac{Nq_{11}}{n_{11}}\right]^{n_{11}} \left[\frac{\theta N q_{22}}{(1-\theta)n_{12}}\right]^{n_{12}} \left[\frac{Nq_{21}}{n_{21}}\right]^{n_{21}}$$

$$\times \left[\frac{Nq_{22}}{n_{22}}\right]^{n_{22}} \tag{6.5b}$$

$$(n_{12} < n_{21}, \; n_{11} > n_{22})$$

$$= \left[\frac{Nq_{11}}{n_{11}}\right]^{n_{11}} \left[\frac{Nq_{12}}{n_{12}}\right]^{n_{12}} \left[\frac{\theta N q_{11}}{(1-\theta)n_{21}}\right]^{n_{21}}$$

$$\times \left[\frac{Nq_{22}}{n_{22}}\right]^{n_{22}} \tag{6.5c}$$

$$(n_{12} > n_{21}, \; n_{11} < n_{22})$$

$$= \left[\frac{Nq_{11}}{n_{11}}\right]^{n_{11}} \left[\frac{Nq_{12}}{n_{12}}\right]^{n_{12}} \left[\frac{\theta N q_{22}}{(1-\theta)n_{21}}\right]^{n_{21}}$$

$$\times \left[\frac{Nq_{22}}{n_{22}}\right]^{n_{22}} \tag{6.5d}$$

$$(n_{12} > n_{21}, \; n_{11} > n_{22})$$

The third remaining parameter (q_{12} or q_{21}) is given by the requirement of summation to unity and is thus a function of θ, e.g. for the first form (6.5a), $q_{21} = 1 - q_{22} - q_{11}/(1-\theta)$. With the constraint substituted in, the function may be maximized over q_{11} and q_{22} to give $MR_B(\theta)$ from which inferences are made. The form of the relative likelihood function used depends on the data observed. This index is analytically very complex, since it has been adopted for empirical sociological reasons and not for simplicity of analysis. In addition, $\hat{\theta}$ given by eqn. (6.1) will not contain all

138

of the information in the data about the mobility, since no sufficient estimate of θ exists.

The index θ takes the value zero for minimum mobility and one for maximum but the value for perfect mobility is not fixed and may lie anywhere between zero and one. This index may be compared with the index α_1' defined above, which from eqns. (3.3) and (3.8) is

$$\hat{\alpha}_1' = \frac{\sqrt{n_{11}n_{22}}}{\sqrt{n_{11}n_{22}} + \sqrt{n_{12}n_{21}}} \tag{6.6}$$

As stated above, this index is zero for maximum mobility and one for minimum but also has value one half for perfect mobility. Since this index varies inversely to θ, it may be called an index of immobility. The index of mobility is α_2' (derived from $\alpha_2 = -\alpha_1$) with maximum likelihood estimate

$$\hat{\alpha}_2' = \frac{\sqrt{n_{12}n_{21}}}{\sqrt{n_{11}n_{22}} + \sqrt{n_{12}n_{21}}} \tag{6.7}$$

which is zero for minimum, 0.5 for perfect, and one for maximum mobility. The resemblance to $\hat{\theta}$ of eqn. (6.1) is evident. The index $\hat{\alpha}_2'$ is the ratio of the geometric mean of the number of sons leaving their father's category in the two directions to the sum of this mean and the geometric mean of the numbers of sons staying in the father's category. The geometric mean arises from the fact that the probabilities q_{ij} are multiplied, not added. Although this index is derived from theoretical considerations of statistical simplicity and the need to use the maximum amount of information in the data, it may be seen to have a sociological interpretation.

Suppose that a sample of individuals is taken at five year intervals to measure the social mobility and to determine if it is changing. Tables 6.1 and 6.2 give the results for two consecutive samples. From eqns. (6.1) and (6.7), the maximum likelihood estimates of the two indices are found to be $\hat{\theta} = 0.26$, $\hat{\alpha}_2' = 0.33$ and $\hat{\theta} = 0.34$, $\hat{\alpha}_2' = 0.39$ respectively for the two tables. From the two values of $\hat{\alpha}_2'$, one may see immediately that the mobility is somewhat less than perfect but considerably greater than minimum. From the values of the indices for the two tables, the mobility appears to have increased in the five year interval between samples. The sociologist wishes to determine if this increase is supported by the data.

TABLE 6.1

The observed distribution of 200 sons in two social categories divided according to the father's social category. Sample at the beginning of a five year period.

		Son		
		1	2	
Father	1	87	13	100
	2	63	37	100
		150	50	200

TABLE 6.2

The observed distribution of 200 sons in two social categories divided according to the father's social category. Sample at the end of a five year period.

		Son		
		1	2	
Father	1	83	17	100
	2	67	33	100
		150	50	200

The determination of plausibility for α_2' is straightforward. The parameter α_1 in the relative likelihood function (3.6) is transformed

$$\alpha_1 = -\log\left[\frac{\alpha_2'}{1-\alpha_2'}\right]$$

and $R_B(\mu,\alpha_2')$ maximized over μ to obtain a graph similar to that of Fig. 3.2. Since this procedure was discussed in detail in Chapter 3, the analysis will not be reapplied here.

The relative likelihood function for θ as given in eqn. (6.5) is much more complex. For the two samples being analyzed, $n_{12} < n_{21}$ and $n_{11} > n_{22}$ so that the second form (6.5b) of $R_M(\theta)$ is used. If this function is maximized over the remaining two parameters and plotted for the two tables, the two graphs are found to overlap greatly. From eqn. (3.22) or (4.8), $R_B(p_{ijk}=\hat{p}_{ik})$ = $MR_B(\theta_1=\theta_2)$ = 0.65 where θ_1 and θ_2 signify the index for the two tables. The calculations and result are exactly the same for α_2' or any other index of mobility with two social categories. This result indicates that the two samples provide no evidence that the

140

mobility has increased in the five year period, *i.e.* it is highly plausible that the mobility has not changed in the period. In order to detect this small change in mobility, a much larger sample would be required.

All of the indices of social mobility traditionally used, including Boudon's, have an inherent drawback related to the discussion in Section 3.2. Usually, samples are taken for fixed numbers of individuals in the sons' categories and the fathers' determined (inverse sampling). This produces a bias in the fathers' generation, as described by Duncan (1966). The values $n_{ik}/n_{.k}$ can be calculated but $n_{ik}/n_{i.}$ is meaningless as is $n_{ik}/n_{..}$. Forms one (6.4a) and four (6.4d) of θ cannot be calculated (are meaningless), since they have the form $n_{ik}/n_{i.}$. For example, if equal numbers of sons in the two social categories are sampled and their fathers' categories determined, one of these two forms necessarily results and Boudon's index is meaningless. But, as shown in Section 3.2, the index (6.7) can still be estimated (and is the only one which can be) and the bias at the fathers' generation, inherent in previous mobility indices, is automatically avoided with α_2'. In summary, the advantages of this index, simplicity of analysis (likelihood function), total use of information, and elimination of bias (applicability of inverse sampling) weigh heavily towards its adoption.

The development of a single index when the number of social categories $K > 2$ is very complex. The initial sociological problem is to decide how to compare the mobility when an individual moves between, say, categories 1 and 2 and between categories 2 and 4. In other words, a metric must be developped to describe the relationship among categories. The simplest, but most unrealistic, assumption is to have equal distances between all pairs of categories. In this case, the generalization of the index θ, derived from an index given by Matras (1960), is immediate from eqn. (6.2). Unfortunately, the relative likelihood function becomes impossibly complex with $K > 2$ so that this index is of little practical use. Similarly, eqn. (6.7) might be generalized by taking the geometric means of all on-diagonal and all off-diagonal elements to yield a value of α_2' for $K > 2$. But, the advantages of this index, simplicity, elimination of bias, and sufficiency (total use of information) are lost.

The next simplest model assumes that the social categories are ordered, with equal distance between consecutive categories. The generalization of θ in this case is derived from an index given by Bartholomew (1967). Formulation in a closed form is not simple,

141

but it can be very easily calculated. For the observed marginal totals, a table with maximum mobility is constructed by placing as many individuals as possible as far as possible from the diagonal and proceeding inward to the diagonal. Conversely, a table with minimum mobility has as many individuals on the diagonal as possible and decreases away from the diagonal. Both of these tables have most entries zero. For the three tables, with maximum, minimum, and observed mobility, the amount of mobility is calculated as $\sum_i \sum_k n_{ik} |i-k|$. In the same way that eqn. (6.2) was constructed, this generalization of $\hat{\theta}$ is the ratio of observed minus minimum mobility to maximum minus minimum. Both of these generalisations reduce to eqn. (6.1) when $K = 2$. If a different metric, say, $g(i,k)$, is defined for differences between social categories, $|i-k|$ is replaced by this metric function in the above index to give the most general case. All of these extensions have the same drawbacks as Boudon's original index, especially that they usually cannot be estimated if an inverse sampling scheme is used.

At the beginning of this section, the relative likelihood function, $R_M(p_{ik}=\hat{p}_k)$, from eqn. (4.2) was suggested as being very useful in analyzing the mobility for $K > 2$ social categories. In the same way, using the methods of Section 4.2, the plausibility of the mobility being the same for a number of samples (such as those at five year intervals in the example given above) may be determined. The response variable is the son's social category, and the two independent variables are the father's category and the sample number. Relative likelihood (4.8) or (4.13), depending on whether interaction occurs between father's category and sample (time), gives the plausibility of mobility being the same.

If the sample of individuals at the end of a five year period is found more plausibly to have perfect mobility than the corresponding sample at the beginning of the period (even if plausibility of perfect mobility is very small in both cases) and if the mobility is found to be plausibly different between samples, the sociologist may conclude that the mobility has plausibly increased in the five years without calculating the values of any index. This procedure has the same advantages as outlined for two social categories with $\alpha_2{}'$ and, in addition, no metric need be adopted among categories nor any condensation of information applied either by reduction to only two social categories or by calculating the value of one index in the presence of many categories. (In effect, $(K-1)^2$ indices are used simultaneously.)

142

6.3 Social Mobility as a Process

In this section, an example is given of a model developed to explain the process by which a son, with father of a given social category, obtains his own category. Suppose that a number of social categories are represented in the sample and that individuals tend to move easily within one of several groups of categories but rarely between groups. Perfect mobility is hypothesized within each group. If K social categories are represented, up to L groups may be hypothesized where

$$L \leqslant \frac{K^2}{2K-1} \tag{6.8}$$

Then, m_{ik}^l represents the number of sons of category k with fathers of category i and belonging to group l (=1,...,L). Since perfect mobility is hypothesized, within the group

$$m_{ik}^l = \frac{m_{i.}^l \, m_{.k}^l}{m_{..}^l} \tag{6.9}$$

where $m_{i.}^l$, $m_{.k}^l$, and $m_{..}^l$ are unknown parameters to be estimated. Since the marginal totals $n_{i.}$ and $n_{.k}$ are assumed fixed (*i.e.* the social structure), the total number of parameters is reduced by the constraints

$$\sum_i m_{i.}^l = \sum_k m_{.k}^l = m_{..}^l$$

$$\sum_l m_{i.}^l = n_{i.}$$

$$\sum_l m_{.k}^l = n_{.k} \tag{6.10}$$

$$\sum_l m_{..}^l = n_{..}$$

Since

$$n_{ik} = \sum_l m_{ik}^l = \sum_l \left[\frac{m_{i.}^l \, m_{.k}^l}{m_{..}^l} \right]$$

these parameters are related to the parameters, p_{ik}, of the multinomial distribution by

$$p_{ik} = \sum_l \left[\frac{m_{i.}^l \, m_{.k}^l}{n_{i.} \, m_{..}^l} \right]$$
(6.11)

which may be substituted into the relative likelihood function
(4.1) to make plausibility statements about the model and about
various parameter values. Unfortunately, the likelihood surface is
very flat, indicating that the values of the parameters in a very
large range are almost equally plausible. In addition, the surface
always contains at least one local relative maximum, making
estimation of parameters even more difficult. The maximum likelihood estimates may be obtained by solving the equations obtained
by setting the partial derivatives of the log (relative) likelihood
function with respect to each parameter equal to zero, as described in Appendix 2. The analysis of this model, including calculation of parameter estimates, is given in detail by Boudon (1973).

A number of simpler versions of this model have been developed, using only two groups ($L = 2$). A model originally proposed
by Blumen *et al.* (1955) for intragenerational mobility, and applied by White (1970) to intergenerational mobility, assumes that
one group of individuals has the same social category as their
fathers while the second group has perfect mobility. Members of
the first group occur only on the diagonal, while those of the
second group occur anywhere in the table. The counts are given by

$$n_{ii} = m_{ii}^1 + m_{i.}^2 m_{.i}^2 / m_{..}^2$$

$$n_{ik} = m_{i.}^2 m_{.k}^2 / m_{..}^2 \qquad (i \neq k)$$

where $m_{ii}^2 = n_{i.} - m_{i.}^2$, $m_{.k}^2 = m_{i.}^2 - n_{i.} + n_{.k}$ so that eqn. (6.11) becomes

$$p_{ii} = \frac{m_{ii}^2}{n_{i.}} + \frac{m_{i.}^2 m_{.i}^2}{m_{..}^2 n_{i.}}$$

$$p_{ik} = \frac{m_{i.}^2 m_{.k}^2}{m_{..}^2 n_{i.}} \qquad (i \neq k)$$
(6.12)

Again, these may be substituted into the relative likelihood function (4.1) in order to obtain maximum likelihood estimates and to

144

make inferences. Since only sums of (and not the individual) off diagonal counts appear in the likelihood function, these estimates are identical to those given by White.

A further simplifying assumption, proposed by Goodman (1961), is that individuals of the second group must move ($m_{ii}^2 = 0$). In this case, eqn. (6.11) becomes

$$p_{ii} = \frac{m_{ii}^1}{n_{i.}}$$

$$p_{ik} = \frac{m_{i.}^2 m_{.k}^2}{m_{..}^2 n_{i.}} \quad (i \neq k)$$

(6.13)

Substitution into the relative likelihood function (4.1) and taking derivatives leads to the maximum likelihood estimates

$$\hat{p}_{ii} = n_{ii}/n_{i.} \quad \text{or} \quad \hat{m}_{ii}^1 = n_{ii}$$

and

$$\hat{p}_{ik} = \frac{(n_{i.} - n_{ii})(n_{.k} - n_{kk})}{(n_{..} - \sum_j n_{jj}) n_{i.}}$$

or

$$\hat{m}_{i.}^2 = n_{i.} - n_{ii}, \quad \hat{m}_{.k}^2 = n_{.k} - n_{kk}, \quad \hat{m}_{..}^2 = n_{..} - n_{jj}$$

Again, inferences are made using the relative likelihood function (4.1). This last model has the serious defect that $\sum_k p_{ik} \neq 1$ (which Goodman corrects by introducing a concept of quasi-perfect mobility), so that it will always have low plausibility of explaining the data well.

Inferences about the models are made in the same way as for models in previous chapters. The corresponding relative likelihood functions with the maximum likelihood estimates are used to compare the relative plausibility of the three models. Generally, the first two models will be more plausible than Goodman's, and the first (Boudon's) more plausible than the second (White's). This results because the two simpler models are special cases of eqn. (6.11) obtained by fixing the values of some of the parameters.

It is interesting to note that these models, as exemplified in general by eqn. (6.11), combine simultaneously a mathematical model and a probability model, using the symmetry of the response and independent variables. As a probability model, eqn. (6.11) links the values $p_{i1}, p_{i2}, p_{i3}, ..., p_{iK}$ for each i and as a mathematical model, it links the sets $(p_{i1}, p_{i2}, ..., p_{iK})$ for all values of i.

Many other more complex statistical models have been and are being developed to describe the process of social mobility. These provide few new problems of statistical inference not presented in this book. Indeed, the complex models are usually statistically quite simple to analyze, their complexity lying in the introduction of a number of sociological factors.

CHAPTER 7

Conclusion

The data available to the sociologist come from two principal types of source: those which cover the entire population of a country, such as government census information and elections, and the much smaller survey samples of a portion of the population. In either case, questions are posed, whether to obtain facts (*e.g.* occupation) or opinion (*e.g.* political preference) and the numbers of individuals responding in different ways are counted. The type of question formulated determines the form which the answer will take. In most cases, the different answers form a nominal or, at most, an ordinal variable. The analysis of the second type of such data has been the subject of this book. (The parameter estimates, but not the inferences, are applicable to comprehensive data for the whole population.)

As the quantitative aspect of sociology becomes more sophisticated, more informative relationships are sought among the variables recorded. With nominal and ordinal data, the basic relationships which may be found only take the form of differences. The sociologist asks how much different is the distribution of responses when an independent variable changes. In effect, this simply summarizes the information in the data and does not describe how the relationship changes. Most of the analyses of Chapters 3 and 4 were concerned with this sort of inference.

An important step can be made if the independent variable has a metric. A smooth mathematical relationship, in the form of a regression equation (Sections 3.6 and 3.7), can be developed in an attempt to explain how the response distribution changes. This can be used, for example, to predict the form of the response

147

distribution under intermediate conditions which were not observed. One of the most important metric variables in sociology is time. In the most elementary case, samples are taken from the population at successive intervals of time (with different individuals from the population usually appearing in each sample) and the response distribution determined. The data from French elections of Section 4.3 is an example of this form. Important books in this field include Cox (1970) for dichotomous data and Draper and Smith (1966) for normally distributed data.

But the method of successive independent sampling in time has drawbacks. The sociologist obtains a picture of how individuals behave at successive points in time, but no information on if and how (groups of) individuals change their responses with time. For example, how many individuals voted four consecutive times for party 1, how many individuals three times for party 1 and then once for party 2, and so on for all possible combinations? If this type of information is available, giving transitions from one response to another, an analysis using stochastic processes may be applied. Unfortunately, this form of information is rarely available to the sociologist, primarily because it is expensive to collect and because it requires a large intrusion into the privacy of the individuals sampled. A major exception to this, social mobility, was discussed briefly in Chapter 6. Feller (1968) and Cox and Miller (1965) give the probability theory for stochastic processes; Jenkins and Watts (1968) provide methods of likelihood inference; and Bartholomew (1967) applications in the social sciences.

The second major step towards more informative description of sociological relationships involves the search for sociologically relevant metric response variables. Several illustrations of the simplest manner by which to accomplish this were given in Chapters 1 and 2. Especially if the individual studied is not a person but a social group, numbers of people in various categories may be counted and used as a metric response. If individual towns are studied, the numbers of suicides, of housewives, etc. are counted; if the individual schools are studied, the numbers of students, of teachers, etc. are counted; and so on. Such discrete response variables may usually be described by more sophisticated probability distributions than the multinomial, with the great advantages gained by reduction to one or two parameters. Both discrete probability distributions and the literature describing them are listed comprehensively in Patil and Joshi (1968) (see also Feller, 1968). Many examples of continuous response variables are also

148

available to the sociologist. Common examples involve time or money: time lost from work, salary, cost of housing, etc. The common continuous probability distributions are described by Feller (1970). No attempt appears to have been made in sociology to describe social responses by probability distributions: what probability function describes the distribution of incomes within a factory? within an age group? within a social class? within a country? Can these distributions be simply related, with the same probability function but different parameter values? After this basic groundwork in probability model building begins, further questions arise. What mathematical model describes the change in income distribution among factories? among age groups? etc. And what stochastic process describes the change with time?

APPENDIX 1

Statistical Inference

With the advent of the electronic computer, and especially in the last few years, a great many changes have been brought about in the statistical analysis of data. Traditionally, a very large part of statistical analysis has involved molding the observed data into a form in which the assumptions of the normal distribution can be assumed to apply at least approximately. A correlation coefficient is applied, a least squares regression curve fitted, or analysis of variance applied. In this way, the very simple mathematical properties of the normal distribution can be used to advantage in performing the required calculations. Because of the central limit theorem and the asymptotic properties of the normal distribution, very often the approximation is sufficiently accurate, especially if a large number of observations are available.

Since the largest part of sociological data collected takes the form of counts of individuals having various characteristics, the first step usually involves taking the proportion or percentage of individuals having each characteristic and then assuming that this number has a normal distribution. If the proportion is near 0.5 and/or if a large number of individuals have been observed, the approximation will be good, but as the proportion diverges from 0.5, the sample size required increases rapidly. But, in addition, a large amount of information has already been lost in forming the proportion: the numbers of individuals involved. This may easily be seen if two proportions are to be combined. Consider combining the proportions $1/7$ and $19/21$. With only the proportions, $(1/7 + 19/21)/2 = 0.52$, whereas with the counts $(1 + 19)/(7 + 21)$ $= 0.71$. Thus, approximations are introduced at two levels: loss of the information in the counts and addition of the normal theory assumptions. With the availability of high-speed electronic computers, the strong assumptions (although often realistic) of normal theory may be relaxed by considering other probability distributions which appear more reasonable for the data at hand.

Several levels of statistical inference are available, depending on the information sought from the data and on the assumptions which the sociologist is willing to make. If the sociologist seeks an interval within which a parameter lies with a certain probability, one of two situations must hold. Either the data must follow one of a very restricted number of distributions (including the normal), in which case a fiducial or a structural probability statement may be made. Or, the very strong assumption of a prior probability distribution of the parameter values must be formulated so that Bayes theorem may be applied to the likelihood function.

If the sociologist has formed an hypothesis about the model *before obtaining the data*, he may wish to determine if the hypothesis is supported by the data or if it must be rejected (without comparison with any other hypothesis: assumptions must be made about the set of all possible outcomes which might have been observed and about the probability of each of these outcomes). A test of significance is applied. Naturally, such a test is not valid if the hypothesis is formed from inspection of the data; the test will then almost invariably show that the data support the hypothesis. Two fundamentally different theories of tests of significance have been advanced, by the Fisherian and the Neyman—Pearson schools, but in most common situations, they provide the same analysis.

A set of data is usually used to form or to refine an hypothesis, which may then be supported or rejected by similar data subsequently collected. It is this third objective of statistical analysis with which this book is concerned: the formation and comparison of hypotheses given a set of data in order to determine the most plausible hypothesis in the light of the observations. To do this, a likelihood analysis is applied. With a computer, the form of the likelihood function under each hypothesis may be investigated in detail given the observed data.

The likelihood function is a point measure of plausibility, unlike the probability function which may be used as an interval measure. One may determine the probability of a given variable lying within some fixed interval given a probability distribution. But, one cannot say that a parameter lies within a fixed interval

151

with some likelihood, only that each parameter value (point) in the interval has at least some minimum value of the relative likelihood function. The likelihood function is used for estimation of parameters in a model and for discrimination among parameter values or models as to plausibility. Another distinct theory of discrimination, the Neyman—Pearson theory of hypothesis testing and confidence intervals, has been developed to analyze this problem. This approach has a number of strong drawbacks, which seem to make it less useful than likelihood inference procedures. Two of these concern use of information and invariance.

The likelihood function contains all of the information in the data about the model; many procedures of Neyman—Pearson theory are not based on the likelihood function and thus do not use all of the information. Inferences are invariant if they remain unchanged when a parameter is transformed, *e.g.* from α_1 to α_1' in Section 3.2. If a confidence interval (d_1, d_2) is found for α_1 and then d_1 and d_2 are transformed as is α_1 to produce α_1' using eqn. (3.8), the interval will not, in general, be the same as that derived directly for α_1' using the same method. In contrast, likelihood inferences use all of the available information and are invariant under transformations. An exception for Neyman—Pearson theory occurs when a likelihood ratio test of significance and the corresponding confidence intervals are used, since these are based on the likelihood function, but the advantage of these over the relative likelihood (ratio) is not evident since asymptotic normality must be assumed.

Kalbfleisch (1971) and Edwards (1972) provide the best introduction to likelihood inference, the first after covering the basic principles of probability theory required. Other examples of the use of the likelihood function in statistical inference were mentioned in the preface and are given in the references.

Numerical Methods

Most of the procedures described in the text may be used for small quantities of data with only the aid of a table of logarithms and a desk calculator. Of course, access to an electronic computer is always desirable. But some of the methods, particularly those of Sections 3.4, 4.3, and 6.3, are virtually impossible without a computer since they require solution of a set of non-linear equations.

Many computer centres have available function maximization programmes which may be used directly to obtain the maximum likelihood estimates by maximizing the likelihood function. But, when these are not available or if the sociologist wishes to develop his own programmes for specialized purposes, the commonly used method for obtaining maximum likelihood estimates is the multi-parameter equivalent of Newton's method.

The basic procedure for obtaining maximum likelihood estimates was outlined in Section 1.3: the first derivatives of the log likelihood function are set to zero and the resulting equations solved. Consider eqn. (3.20) of Section 3.4. The log likelihood equation is

$$\log L(\mu, \alpha_i, \gamma_{ij}) = \mu n_{..1} + \sum_i \alpha_i n_{i.1} + \sum_i \sum_j \gamma_{ij} n_{ij1} -$$

$$\sum_i \sum_j n_{ij.} \log[1 + \exp(\mu + \alpha_i + \gamma_{ij})]$$

with first derivatives

$$\frac{\partial}{\partial\mu}: \quad n_{..1} - \sum_i \sum_j \left[\frac{n_{ij.}\ \exp(\hat{\mu}+\hat{\alpha}_i+\hat{\gamma}_{ij})}{1+\exp(\hat{\mu}+\hat{\alpha}_i+\hat{\gamma}_{ij})}\right] = 0$$

$$\frac{\partial}{\partial\alpha_i}: \quad n_{i.1} - \sum_i \left[\frac{n_{ij.}\ \exp(\hat{\mu}+\hat{\alpha}_i+\hat{\gamma}_{ij})}{1+\exp(\hat{\mu}+\hat{\alpha}_i+\hat{\gamma}_{ij})}\right] + \hat{\delta}_1 = 0 \qquad (i=1,...,I)$$

$$\frac{\partial}{\partial\gamma_{ij}}: \quad n_{ij1} - \frac{n_{ij.}\ \exp(\hat{\mu}+\hat{\alpha}_i+\hat{\gamma}_{ij})}{1+\exp(\hat{\mu}+\hat{\alpha}_i+\hat{\gamma}_{ij})} + \hat{\delta}_{2j} + \hat{\delta}_{3i} = 0 \qquad \begin{array}{l}(i=1,...,I;\\ j=1,...,J)\end{array}$$

The significance of $\hat{\delta}_1$, $\hat{\delta}_{2j}$, and $\hat{\delta}_{3i}$ will be explained below. These equations are non-linear in the parameters and cannot be solved directly. An iterative procedure may be used to find successively closer approximations to the estimates. In addition, the constraints on the mathematical model imply that some parameters are redundant. In the simple case of eqn. (3.20), these may be eliminated by substitution. But, in general, this complicates greatly the problem of taking derivatives. An additional term, containing a Lagrange multiplier, may be added to the log likelihood function for each constraint. In this example, the terms added are

$$\delta_1(\sum_i\alpha_i-0) + \sum_j(\delta_{2j}\sum_i\gamma_{ij}-0) + \sum_i(\delta_{3i}\sum_j\gamma_{ij}-0)$$

Hence, the additional parameters (Lagrange multipliers), δ_1, δ_{2j}, and δ_{3i}, to be estimated, appear in the derivatives given above. Additional first derivatives must be taken for each of these parameters.

$$\frac{\partial}{\partial\delta_1}: \quad \sum_i\hat{\alpha}_i = 0$$

$$\frac{\partial}{\partial\delta_{2j}}: \quad \sum_i\hat{\gamma}_{ij} = 0 \qquad (j=1,...,J)$$

$$\frac{\partial}{\partial\delta_{3i}}: \quad \sum_j\hat{\gamma}_{ij} = 0 \qquad (i=1,...,I)$$

Newton's method also requires the calculation of all second-order partial derivatives.

$$\frac{\partial^2}{\partial\mu^2}, \frac{\partial^2}{\partial\alpha_i^2}, \frac{\partial^2}{\partial\mu\partial\alpha_i}, \frac{\partial^2}{\partial\alpha_i\partial\alpha_k}, \frac{\partial^2}{\partial\gamma_{ij}\partial\delta_1}, \text{ etc.}$$

154

When this has been done, an initial estimate is chosen for each parameter (the Lagrange multipliers are usually given initial values of zero) and substituted into the expressions for the first and second derivatives, giving a numerical value for each. The numerical values of the first-order partial derivatives may be placed in a vector $\mathbf{F}$.

$$\mathbf{F} = \left[\frac{\partial}{\partial\mu}, \frac{\partial}{\partial\alpha_1}, ..., \frac{\partial}{\partial\alpha_I}, \frac{\partial}{\partial\gamma_{11}}, ..., \frac{\partial}{\partial\gamma_{IJ}}, \frac{\partial}{\partial\delta_1}, ...\right]$$

and the corresponding second-order derivatives in a matrix $\mathbf{S}$.

$$\mathbf{S} = \begin{bmatrix} \frac{\partial^2}{\partial\mu^2}, \frac{\partial^2}{\partial\mu\partial\alpha_1}, ..., \frac{\partial^2}{\partial\mu\partial\alpha_I}, \frac{\partial^2}{\partial\mu\partial\gamma_{11}}, ..., \frac{\partial^2}{\partial\mu\partial\gamma_{IJ}}, \frac{\partial^2}{\partial\mu\partial\delta_1}, ... \\[2ex] \frac{\partial^2}{\partial\mu\partial\alpha_1}, \frac{\partial^2}{\partial\alpha_1^2}, ..., \frac{\partial^2}{\partial\alpha_1\partial\alpha_I}, \frac{\partial^2}{\partial\alpha_1\partial\gamma_{11}}, ..., \frac{\partial^2}{\partial\alpha_1\partial\gamma_{IJ}}, \frac{\partial^2}{\partial\alpha_1\partial\delta_1}, ... \\[2ex] ... \quad ... \quad ... \quad ... \quad ... \quad ... \quad ... \quad ... \quad ... \end{bmatrix}$$

with the same order for the parameters in the matrix as in the vector. Similarly, the initial estimates form a vector $\mathbf{E}_1$.

$$\mathbf{E}_1 = (\mu^1, \alpha_1^1, ..., \alpha_I^1, \gamma_{11}^1, ..., \gamma_{IJ}^1, \delta_1^1, ...)$$

again in the same order. The new estimates in the vector $\mathbf{E}_2$

$$\mathbf{E}_2 = (\mu^2, \alpha_1^2, ..., \alpha_I^2, \gamma_{11}^2, ..., \gamma_{IJ}^2, \delta_1^2, ...)$$

are given by

$$\mathbf{E}_{i+1} = \mathbf{E}_i - \mathbf{F}\mathbf{S}^{-1}$$

where $\mathbf{S}^{-1}$ is the inverse of the matrix $\mathbf{S}$. (The diagonal elements of this inverse matrix at the final iteration step provide the variance estimates for the parameters mentioned in Section 3.7). The new estimates in the vector $\mathbf{E}_2$ replace the initial estimates in $\mathbf{E}_1$ and the process is repeated until all of the estimates at two successive iterations are sufficiently close together. These values are the required maximum likelihood estimates. A criterion of convergence which provides three or four significant figures is usually adequate within the limitations of the data and the computer.

This general procedure may be applied to any of the models discussed in the text. (If no constraints are present, the Lagrange multipliers are omitted.)

155

The same procedure is used to plot a maximum relative likelihood graph for a parameter. The parameter for which the graph is to be plotted is set at some value and the first- and second-order partial derivatives of the log likelihood function found for all of the remaining parameters. This is equivalent to eliminating the parameter from the vectors E_i and F and the corresponding row and column from the matrix S. Good initial estimates are usually the overall maximum likelihood estimates previously obtained. The iteration procedure is followed to convergence and the values of the parameters so obtained, along with the fixed value of the parameter of interest, are substituted into the relative likelihood function to give a point on the graph. The process is repeated with other values of the parameter until the form of the curve is evident (perhaps 20 or 30 points). If successive values of the parameter are taken in order, good initial estimates for each stage are the final values of the previous stage. Since the estimates change slowly as one parameter is changed, convergence is rapid at each stage.

Computer programmes for some of the models of Chapters 2 and 3 are available in Lindsey (1971) using this method.

References

Barnard, G.A., G.M. Jenkins and C.B. Winsten, (1962). "Likelihood Inferences and Time Series," *J. Royal Statistical Soc.*, Ser. A 125, 321—372.

Bartholomew, D.J. (1967). *Stochastic Models for Social Processes.* New York: Wiley.

Blalock, H.M. (1962a). "Four-variable Causal Models and Partial Correlations," *Amer. J. Sociol.* 68, 182—194.

Blalock, H.M. (1962b). "Further Observations on Asymmetric Causal Models," *Amer. Sociol. Rev.* 27, 539—548.

Blalock, H.M. (1964). *Causal Inferences in Nonexperimental Research.* Chapel Hill: University of North Carolina Press.

Blalock, H.M. (1971) ed. *Causal Models in the Social Sciences.* London: MacMillan.

Bliss, C.I. (1967). *Statistics in Biology.* New York: McGraw-Hill.

Blumen, I., M. Kogan and P.J. McCarthy (1955). "The Industrial Mobility of Labor as a Probability Process," *Cornell Studies of Industrial and Labor Relations*, Vol. VI, New York State School of Industrial and Labor Relations, Cornell University, Ithaca, New York.

Boudon, R. (1970). *L'Analyse Mathématique des Faits Sociaux.* 2nd edn., Paris: Plon.

Boudon, R. (1971). *Les Mathématiques en Sociologie.* Paris: Presses Universitaires de France.

Boudon, R. (1973). *Mathematical Structures of Social Mobility.* Amsterdam: Elsevier.

Box, G.E.P. and D.R. Cox (1964). "An Analysis of Transformations," *J. Royal Statistical Soc.*, Ser. B 26, 211—252.

Cochran, W.G. and G.M. Cox (1966). *Experimental Designs.* 2nd edn., New York: Wiley.

Cox, D.R. (1966). "A Simple Example of a Comparison Involving Quantal Data," *Biometrika* 53, 215—220.

Cox, D.R. (1970). *The Analysis of Binary Data.* London: Methuen.

Cox, D.R. and H.D. Miller (1965). *The Theory of Stochastic Processes.* London: Methuen.

Draper, N.R. and H. Smith (1966). *Applied Regression Analysis*. New York: Wiley.

Duncan, O.D. (1966). "Methodological Issues in the Analysis of Social Mobility," in Smelser, N. and Lipset, S., eds., *Social Structures and Mobility in Economic Development*, pp.51—97. Chicago: Aldine.

Edwards. A.W.F. (1972). *Likelihood: An Account of the Statistical Concept of Likelihood and Its Application to Scientific Inference*. Cambridge: Cambridge University Press.

Feller, W. (1968). *An Introduction to Probability Theory and its Applications*, Vol. I, 3rd edn., New York: Wiley.

Feller, W. (1970). *An Introduction to Probability Theory and its Applications*, Vol. II, 2nd edn., New York: Wiley.

Fisher, R.A. (1959a). *Statistical Methods and Scientific Inference*, 2nd edn., Edinburgh: Oliver & Boyd.

Fisher, R.A. (1959b). *Smoking — The Cancer Controversy*. Edinburgh: Oliver & Boyd.

Fisher, R.A. and F. Yates (1963). *Statistical Tables*. 6th edn., Edinburgh: Oliver & Boyd.

Gart, J.J. (1971). "The Comparison of Proportions: a Review of Significance Tests, Confidence Intervals, and Adjustments for Stratification," *Bull. Intern. Statistical Inst.* 48, 148—169.

Goodman, L. (1961). "Statistical Methods for a Mover—Stayer Model," *J. Amer. Statistical Assoc.* 56, 841—868.

Goodman, L. (1972). "A General Model for the Analysis of Surveys," *Amer. J. Sociol.* 77, 1035—1086.

Grizzle, J.E. and O.D. Williams (1972). "Log Linear Models and Tests of Independence for Contingency Tables," *Biometrics* 28, 137—156.

Jenkins, G.M. and D. Watts (1968). *Analysis of Time Series*. San Francisco: Holden-Day.

Kalbfleisch, J.D. and D.A. Sprott (1970). "Applications of Likelihood Methods to Models Involving Large Numbers of Parameters," *J. Royal Statistical Soc., Ser. B* 32, 175—208.

Kalbfleisch, J.G. (1971). *Probability and Statistical Inference*. Department of Statistics, University of Waterloo, Waterloo, Canada.

Lazarsfeld, P.F. (1955). "The Interpretation of Statistical Relations as a Research Operation," in Lazarsfeld, P.F. and Rosenberg, M., eds., *The Language of Social Research*. pp.115—125. New York: The Free Press.

Lazarsfeld, P.F. (1968). "Survey Analysis: the Analysis of Attribute Data," in Sills, D.L., ed., *International Encyclopedia of the Social Sciences*. Vol. 15, pp.419—428. New York: Collier and MacMillan.

Lindsey, J.K. (1971). *Programs for the Analysis of Non-normal Data*. Fisheries Research Board of Canada Tech. Report 275.

Lindsey, J.K. (1973). "Comparison of Probability Distributions," *J. Royal Statistical Soc., Ser. B* 35, in press.

Lindsey, J.K. and F.W. Nash (1972). "Likelihood Analysis of Three-way Contingency Tables," *J. Fisheries Res. Board Canada* 29,590—591.

Lombard, H.L. and C.R. Doering (1947). "Treatment of the Four-fold Table by Partial Correlation as it Relates to Public Health Problems," *Biometrics* 3, 123—128.

Matras, J. (1960). "Differential Fertility, Intergenerational Occupational

Mobility and Change in the Occupational Distribution: some Elementary Interrelationships," *Population Studies* 15, 187—197.

Patil, G.P. and S.W. Joshi (1968). *A Dictionary and Bibliography of Discrete Distributions.* Edinburgh: Oliver & Boyd.

Rasch, G. (1960). *Probabilistic Models for Some Intelligence and Attainment Tests.* Copenhagen: Nielson and Lydiche.

Rasch, G. (1961). "On General Laws and the Meaning of Measurement in Psychology," *Proc. 4th Berkeley Symp.* 4, 321—333.

Robson, D.S. (1959). "A Simple Method for Constructing Orthogonal Polynomials when the Independent Variable is Unequally Spaced," *Biometrics* 15, 187—191.

Simon, H.A. (1954). "Spurious Correlation: a Causal Interpretation," *J. Amer. Statistical Assoc.* 49, 467—479.

Sonquist, J.A. and J.N. Morgan (1963). "Problems in Analysis of Survey Data and a Proposal," *J. Amer. Statistical Assoc.* 58, 415—434.

Sprott, D.A. (1964). "Uses of Chi-square," *J. Abnormal and Social Psychology* 69, 101—103.

Sprott, D.A. and J.D. Kalbfleisch (1969). "Examples of Likelihoods and Comparison with Point Estimates and Large Sample Approximations," *J. Amer. Statistical Assoc.* 64, 468—484.

Sprott, D.A. and J.G. Kalbfleisch (1965). "Use of the Likelihood Function in Inferences," *Psychology Bull.* 64, 15—22.

Torgerson, W.S. (1958). *Theory and Methods of Scaling.* New York: Wiley.

White, H. (1970). "Stayers and Movers," *Amer. J. Sociol.* 76, 307—324.

Index

161

model, see probability model, mathematical model
multidimensional scaling, 3, 44-45

nominal data, see data, variable

occupation, 44-45
order, 3, 11, 16, 22, 85, 91
ordinal data, see data, variable
orthogonal polynomials, 91, 111, see also regression
outcomes, see counts, parameters (reduction by combination), variables

parameter, infinite number, 12
  large numbers of, 98, 102-103, 120-122
  nuisance, 97, 120-122
  plausibility of being zero, 71-72, 92-94, 107
  reduction, by combination, 11, 29-45, 124, 133
    inferences, 18, 49, 54, 56, 73-75, 78-80, 102-103, 117-118
    by setting to zero, 71-81, 84-85, 90-94, 108-111, 113-115, 118
    by transformation, 8-10, 22-25, 115-116
  theoretical values, 50, 54-56, 94-95
  transformation, 66-67, 152
path analysis, ix-xi
Patil and Joshi, 148
population, 6-11, 19, 28, 46, 111-112, 147
precision, of inferences, within model, 71-72, 80-81, 83, 93-94, 107
  and sample size, 14-15, 65, 81
  see also sample
  of measuring device, 5, 28-29, 46-47
  see also interval widths, unit of measurement
probability model, building, 10-11, 45-49, 148-149
  multivariate, 112-114, 118, 145-146

162

normal, 47-49
Poisson, 17-19
see also distribution
pupils attending school, 40-41, 47-54

questionnaire, analysis, 5-8, 11-12, 20, 28-29
  example, 72-78, 91, 103-104, 121-122
  multivariate example, 115-117

random sample, see sample
Rasch, 23, 121
reduction, see information, parameters, variables
regression, binomial, 23, 85-88, 91-93
  general, 27, 147-148
  "least squares" (normal theory), ix-x, 27, 82
  multinomial, 111
  Poisson, 26-27
  see also orthogonal polynomials
relative likelihood function, binomial, 14-16, 22, 60, 63, 71, 75
  maximum, 63-65, 117-118, 120-121, 132
  multinomial, 16, 20-21, 53-54, 98-101, 106, 125-126
  multivariate, 113, 138
  normal, 48
  plotting, 63-65, 77-78, 80, 156
  Poisson, 18-19, 25-26
response, see variable
Robson, 91

salary, 2, 149
samples, combination of, 50-54, 103-104
  general, 6-7, 14-16, 20, 28, 46-47, 111-112, 147
  inverse, 62, 141
  random, 6, 28, 58-59, 82-83
  size, and inference precision, 14-15, 65, 81, 101, 140-141
    and population size, 19, 111-112
saturated model, see mathematical model
scaling, 3